A William Maidment Garland

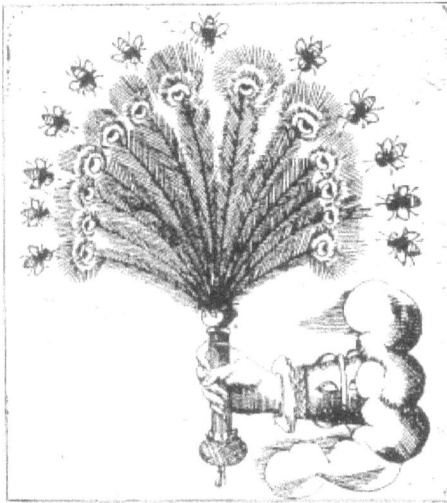

By the same author

A First Reader (2003)
Montale: A Biographical Anthology (2006)
Erasure Traces (2008)
Views of Mount Brogden and a Dictionary of Minor Poets (2008)
Four Refrains (2011)
Occam's Aftershave (2012)
Three Painters (2014)

A William Maidment Garland

Collected Works Volume 6

John Watson

PUNCHER & WATTMANN

First published in 2018

Published by Puncher and Wattmann
PO Box 441
Glebe NSW 2037

http://www.puncherandwattmann.com
puncherandwattmann@bigpond.com

National Library of Australia
Cataloguing-in-Publication entry:

Watson, John

A William Maidment Garland: Collected Works Volume 6

ISBN   9781922186867

I. Title.

A821.3

Cover design by Sophie Gaur

Cover: © Kenji Hoshi /Adobe Stock

Printed by Lightning Source International
This project has been assisted by the
Australian Government through the
Australian Council, its arts funding and
advisory body.

Australian Government

Australia Council
for the Arts

Contents

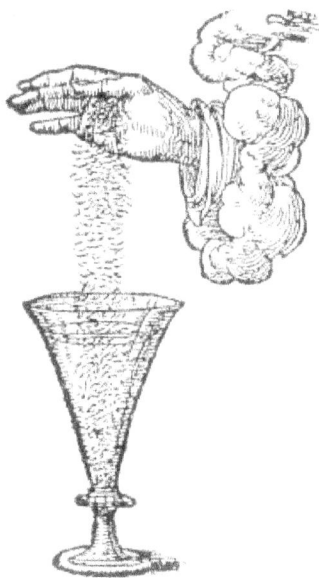

Introduction

He resembled in his smile and features the famous bust of Voltaire. The Smile of Reason was in Bill curiously augmented with a sweetness, a capacity for nostalgia, and a gentleness which made his advocacy of Menippean satire the more subtle and complex. He had seemingly read everything: in the year before his death he re-read all of *Paradise Lost* and *The Fairy Queen*. He was interested in fundamental questions in aesthetics and criticism, particularly in the notion of mimesis; here he took issue with John Anderson (who nonetheless is, with Max Meldrum, one of the presiding spirits intervening with approval in *Confetti*). His clear-sighted judgment was accompanied by modesty and reserve.

He was important to many of us. Perhaps it was the smile, patient yet expectant, which led us to whatever achievements or excesses we might attempt.

What follows are the traces of tribute. *A Peal of Bells*, a 70th birthday poem, had its origins on the day when, from the 4th floor landing in Fisher Library, I saw Bill at the exit turn back, as one of the large satchel of books he had borrowed set off bells.

Confetti is more personal and was written for Bill and Marcia's Golden Wedding. Celebrations included a gathering of admirers beside a cave on the cliffs overlooking Sydney Harbour. The section, *A Family Album*, is a sort of pocket history and may contain obscurities which, I hope, are incidental and benign.

The convalescence poem and *Entropy* were intended as beguilements or distractions, excessively over-long get-well cards, intended for posting. In both, elaboration is the generator and they range over subjects which are often the result of long conversations at his house at the appropriately named Hercules Street.

Memorial was written after Bill's death and is an attempt to explain our loss. The author of *The Leopard* is invoked, pictured at his café table every morning at breakfast, surrounded by the drafts of his celebrated novel. He is a figure suggestive of Bill in several ways: he lectured brilliantly but published little; he had a prodigious knowledge of English Literature; he resisted limelight; he was acutely open to nostalgia.

Gryll Grange is the last novel of Thomas Love Peacock, written many years after the others. In it the Smile of Reason is at its most generous. Peacock was one of Bill's acclaimed authors, in many ways resembling him in his delight in comic seriousness and wide-ranging discussion. *Gryll Grange* is a romance, albeit rendered with highly intelligent amusement. In this it evokes William Maidment, who in his life and work so judiciously combined affection and intellectual discipline. This playful synopsis which concludes the *Garland* was written as a tribute to him (and entertainment for him) but was sadly preceded by his death.

A Peal of Bells

Prefatory Introduc-
tion or Introductory
Preface — They order, said I. Shall we order?
The waitress, Alice, with chocolate mousse
And a menu of dishes in other languages
Bent low over us as we were reading
A collation drawn from sundry sources.
Alice said, — What is the use of a book
Without pictures or conversations?
— This is a cerebration, said the mandarin.
— A macaronic pasta, please, said the sultana.
— And, in between, let us converse
And let us rejoice and rehearse each use
Of the auxiliary verbs. — With herbs
And plentiful garnishes let us have
Variety, sweet variety, zeugma the essence
Of multiplicity, hence of art. Example:
'She looked across the harbour and
A million dollars.' — I'll have, quoth I,
To quaff, the didactic soup. — With sippets?
— A hoddle-poddle, hotch-potch or mish-mash?
— With snippets of other men's flowers.

Tradition and the
Individual Talent — Is this not derivativeness, said Alice,
Yesterdays coldly furnished forth?
— Sir, quoth my uncle Toby, let every man
Tell his story in his own way.

A Secondary Theme — And a soupçon of the Aristotelian
Main dish with a view to sampling
The infinite variety of desserts ranged
Round it like irrigated flowering deserts,
In all directions the universe
Finite but unbounded or is it
Infinite but bounded? The waitress
Bounded to our side. — Sirs,
We are expecting an event of some moment

The Theme

After this repast which is mere preface.
— Would you please welcome —
— We are expecting the appearance of —
— A bumper for Bill!
— A Bumper Annual for Bill!
— We'll repair to the library forecourt,
Said Alice, as one speaking in a palace,
So that when I stretched out my hand to raise my glas

A Gasp of Air

Someone shouted, — Be a football
To time and chance. And we were in the vast
Outdoors with conversation our only support,
Columns and pillars elevating the heavens.
And someone was going on and on
In a circular fashion about being caught flagrantly
With someone delectable in a revolving door. Then

The Nod in the
Direction Pastoral

We were suddenly out in the light
Where a grove of expectant trees had been
Standing since dawn, umbelliferous
Disorder the source of all beauty.
— The person at large in the flux
May be likened to the planetary model
Of matter itself, the Aristotelian unity

The Secondary
Theme Explored

Its nucleus, and round it the great
Corridor of discussion which corresponds
To the probability haze of a handful
Of electrons. Alice ran after us

A Pun Question-
able in the Circum-
stances

Into the high-heeled street. — Sirs, your bill!
The word echoed pleasantly in the world.
But a strange quickening of events
Was underway, at the approaching comet
Of that birthday we were gathered to see
Touched off like a Catherine Wheel.

A Pause and a
Serious Beginning A crowd of us had gathered by the tethering rails
Outside the library, there to catch a glimpse
And shake the hand, if that were feasible
Granted the press and weight of numbers assembled,
Of William Maidment who was today dressing up
As Neptune and crossing the International Date Line
Into his eighth decade. There was a considerable
Jostling; the warmth of esteem met the hush
Of expectation. The first Mexican wave
Passed down this fair field of folk. Then
Banners were raised, anticipating his appearance
On the balcony of history to much applause.
Brightly the balustrades waved their signs:

Protestations of
Well Wishers "Widow Wadman Wishes You Well.
Come up and see me some time";
"Greetings from Gallimaufrical Glasgow";
"Twenty five thousand days bathing
In a warm wash of words"; "Roll on thou deep
And dark blue ocean"; "Yo"; "Excelsior";
"At the dog's bone of letters let us gnaw";
"Books give not wisdom where was none before
But where some is, there reading makes it more";
"To the eighth decade and all who sail in her";
"Irascible Rasselas, where are you now
That we need you?" Then through our throng

A Stranger A stranger approached and asked us, − Sirs,
What manner of man is this who so enthrals
This great assembly that they will hourly wait
His appearance on the battlements? Is he
The scourge of mediocrity, the cleanser
Of the temple, excoriating the pallid
Wherever it raises its head and lopping off
That head and then the two and four and twenty

Which grow in its place? Or is he

A Dilemma

The snapper-up of unconsidered trifles,
Favouring these with the rich custard of applause
And the sprinkled nuts of interest and curiosity,
At pains to point out every slight eminence
On the drought plains of a text,
Generous to a fault, benign, persistent
As my uncle Toby's wound? – Well, yes

Indecision

And no. I mean, what is jesting
Definition? Who is sylvan?

Johnson Enlisted

Remember, in this connection, Johnson, and
I quote: 'Sometimes, things may be
Made darker by definition. I see a cow.
I define her Animal quadrupes
Ruminans cornutam. But a goat
Ruminates and a cow may have
No horns. Cow is plainer.'
Thus the difficulties at this time
In my leaping to either bank
Of your dichotomy, and falling between them
Like the ill-fated Colossus of Rhodes.

A Clamour of Voices Then others said, taking up the torch,
– Not firing mortars from an ivory tower ...
– Contempt for cant and scant regard for Kant ...
– No Garboesque Leavisalones ... – The famous

Faults He Eschewed *No! In Thunder* made Arcadian
With April Showers ... – His was not
The severe practice of the exclusive
And its personalised number-plate EFFOFF
Disappearing down the highway ahead of us ...
– Nor had he truck with the assertion
Of a nit-picking fractious fractal dissolving
Into infinity ... – Lichtenberg's 'moral backside'

He ensured covered by the 'trousers of decorum'

Johnson Ubiquitous – Living in glass houses he don't kick stones.

– I agree with the first speaker.

Another stood on a box to address us:

– He tried to give us all a better view,

Clearing the log–jam at the waterfall

Of seminal works (while never losing sight

Of any one particular log).

Johnson
Omnipresent In this he was like that most sleight

And agile Dr Johnson who,

At the artificial waterfall

(Which Dr Taylor had shored up,

Damming a river in his garden),

Leapt with a heavy wielding pole

And cleared locked branches and, at that,

A swelled, obstructive, large, dead cat

Johnson's Lack of
Condition (Though Johnson out of breath had help

From Boswell to dislodge the cat).

At this the fall could be admired;

That curtain every man desired

Now unimpeded, calmly flowed.

An Odious Com-
parison Averted – But wait, another cried with an interpolation,

Brewer tells how Irish rats were once

Subdued and scattered by the chanting

Of metrical verse! Therefore

Let us be expansive and not set Bill,

On this festive day,

In such a company.

Rather let us give him every benefit of

A Tabula Rasa the
Best Gift Delicious doubt, be as unspecific and liberal,

As unregulated and free, as befits

This auspicious time, and not present him

With any resolution or definition or decision
Or determination any more binding,
Nor let anything *fait* be any more *accompli*,
Than the blank Chapter XVIII
Of the last volume of *Tristram Shandy*
Where My Uncle Toby Visits The Widow Wadman.
The stranger said, – I thank you. I feel the rare
Zest of the air, the spray fresh in my face
From the breaking wave of this joyful moment
And the imminence of his arrival here;
But I have heard, so far, much
That he is not, much that is tendentious,
Allusive, if alluring, and tangential. I would like
To hear some attempt at encompassing,
Or encapsulating all that he is. At this
A courtier in rich attire
Took up the gage and, clearing his throat
A Brief Curriculum Replied in alphabetic mode: – He is
Affable yet adamant,
Buoyant, benign,
Cogitative and cognoscent,
Dictionarian, diaphanous to the light of fact,
Edificative, elucubrationary,
Fabulously fruitful and fruitive,
Genial, generous, gustful and Grandisonian.
He is happily heterodox,
Igniferous,
Jocund,
Kindly, kindling,
Mettlesome and meteoric, metaphoric,
Needling and nettle-grasping,
Occam's Razored and obdurate (where appropriate),
Preceptorial, pluralistic and

Quintessential, quick and quippy. He is
Recondite, rutilant,
Sprag,
Tonitruous and torpedinous (to defend truth),
Ungainsayable but undercumstumbling,
Vital,
Wittily wise,
Yare, yarnspinning,
Zealous and Zenonian.
– Yes, said the stranger, but …

At this, a further quickening of events:
At the library's automatic–opening doors
A woman with her arms filled with dahlias
Paused, as if, having studied too many Empiricists,
She were uncertain whether her substantiality
Might be sufficient to operate the sensor
And open the doors. The thought occurred
Also that she might yet bypass,
By the simple act of thought, causality,
'The cement of the world'. Yet the doors
Opened and the resultant breeze, expelled
By the airconditioning draft, fluttered
Petals from the dahlias to the ground.
A bird was singing, singing
Its own One Note Samba.
A cyclist was slowing his bicycle
To a wobble. The Lady of the Dahlias said
To the world in general and the cyclist in particular
– Observe this stately crowd gathered here
For W. Maidment and his entry
On to the high lake of his seventieth year;
He who taught us to read, to disintricate

Developments

Philosophical
Doubts

Sundry Events

Without reduction or loss, for him
I have cast down these petals ...   There was
A moment of indecision. Then the world
Felt replete, like an ablative absolute,
All having been made in readiness
For his arrival within the hour.
And almost at once there was an unlikely

Suggestions of a
Mysterious Subplot Quickening of events. Alice inexplicably
Came out into the cloud-chamber of the yard.
The sun was photographing every proceeding.
She had exchanged her apron for a white
Ensemble with matching bolero
And colour-co-ordinated parasol.
Unexpectedly she approached the stranger, and

One Last Delay 'Flinging her arms about him' embraced him.
At length she stepped back and said
To him and to all of us, – Now I hope
You haven't let them all go on
Too long and get carried away
With the enticements of narrative. I know
Bill would not want that kind of excess.

A Curious Practice The library doors opened once more. A wave
Like the energy in an uncoiled rope
Snaked out across the expectant crowd
Agog in their compound, waiting a sign.
One of the library staff, the one with long red hair
Who, serenely bemused, looked like those
Several disciples of the twelve
Given merely walk-on parts, walked out
With a trolley of books into the sunlit court.
Someone confided, – They do this with the books,
Or a number of them, on this day

18

Each year. It is thought that these texts,
Absorbing the sun, then burgeon and ripen
As a peach or melon ripens and mellows.

Fulfilment

But now our jubilant patience
Would soon be rewarded. The doors
Opened. The sound of cannon mingled with
The roar of traffic from the metropolis.
Bells were ringing. William Maidment
Appears – but briefly – in the doorway.

A Slight Technical
Hiatus

As bells continue to ring he disappears
Back into the gloom to re-desensitise
One book which librarians smilingly
In the spirit of these celebrations
Have left still charged, thereby to add,
To this glissade of bells, their own. Soon
He reappears, in triumph on the ziggurat,
Unbowed, bearing bundles of books.
Euphoria is general and unconfined.

A Vision

Now the clouds, which must, it seems, carry
A burden of baroque visitations, took the form
Of towers, watering places, hot springs,
Temples, carriages, topiaries. Here,
In the cornucopian hammock of clouds,
Appeared briefly a number of notables,
Worthies, long-familiars, ramblers, spectators, idlers,
Who, as if leaning from some closed barouche,
Called out in one voice their greeting. – Sir,
We have been reading this day
From a projected supplement to a continuation
Of the Tristra-paedia and are therefore
Glad of this opportunity to desist.

We rejoice to take this opportunity
To congratulate you and thank you, Sir,
Who are one of our finest Readers ever,
Penetrant, assiduous, acute, Universal,
In whom we subsist, inhere, may travel still;
To our journeys to the Hebrides, and Abyssinia,
And The Whole Island of Great Britain, and France,
And Italy, and Portugal, and Ireland,
We may add the pleasant perambulations
Made possible through your perusals.
But, Sir, we detain you from your guests.
Of all Appearances such as now we contrive
To greet you on this day, the Metempsychosal,
Visionary and Metaphysical were best made brief.
Touching that subject, one of our number here
Now voices the sentiment, all too often honoured
In the breach: *Length is my greatest Disgust*,
(Who himself tolerably well overcame such distaste
In epistolary fictions of heroic proportions),
So that, even as our warm light reaches you,
In our legion, Sir, we salute you, and depart.

As arrow-forms of lorikeets
Against the dazzling cirrus sky
Fly overhead in their salutes,

Eliza, Stella, Jenny, Alice,
Bright-eyed, high-heeled, amongst us ply
With trays of wine and orange juice.

Hours later in the silver field
The admiring crowds still press to graze,
And dusk at last couches with gold

The multiple and tangling threads
Of conversations laced with praise,
Until the lawns glisten with webs

Of laughter, hope and reveries.
The lawn's an orchard. Here we meet
To share the proffered, ripened fruit
Of pleached and grafted reading years.

IVNGIT AMOR.

Confetti, to Honour the
Golden Wedding of Bill
and Marcia Maidment

She looked very beautifull with some red roses
In her hat and the dainty red ruge in her cheeks
Looked quite the thing. Bernard heaved a sigh
And his eyes flashed as he beheld her
And Ethel thought to herself
What a fine type of manhood he represented.
Bernard sat beside her in a profound silence
Gazing at her pink face and long wavy eye lashes.
Ethel he murmured in a trembling voice.

¤

— I am half distracted Captain Shandy
said Mrs Wadman, holding up her cambrick handkerchief
to her left eye, as she approached the door
of my uncle Toby's sentry-box — a mote —
of sand — or something — I know not what,
has got into this eye of mine — do look into it…

In vain! — Widow Wadman's left eye
shines this moment as lucid as her right —
there is neither mote, or sand, or dust, or chaff,
or speck or particle of opake matter floating in it
— There is nothing my dear paternal uncle
but one lambent delicious fire furtively shooting out
from every part of it in all directions into thine —
If thou lookest, uncle Toby, in search of this mote
one moment longer —thou art undone.

¤

One further pleasure of the married life
From Samuel Pepys (iambically enhanced):

"What great delight we married people take
To see poor fools decoyed into our state."

¤

Oh what is it said Ethel hastily sitting up.
Words fail me ejaculated Bernard horsley
My passion for you is intense
He added fervently. It has grown
Day and night since I first beheld you
Oh said Ethel in surprise I am not
Prepared for this and she lent back
Against the trunk of the tree.
Bernard placed one arm tightly round her.

¤

Spring, 1950. Seams of golden light
Prefigure in that flushed September sky
This rich-veined glowing day.

The harbour stirs and yields its resonant cry.
We seem to hear the voice of Norman May
In exultation: Gold! Gold! Gold!

Just three years (almost to the day)
Since our dear Queen and Duke stood hand in hand
For better or for worse

(Who in their progeny have fared, alas,
In some ways rather worse than better) — then
Today's gold medallists stood on the blocks

About to join the swim. But for these two,
No such *annus horribilis.* When Grave,
Enthusiastic Doubt weds Gaiety,

The years disclose a rich alluvial seam
Of happiness. And so we gather here
To raise on high this Welcome Stranger lode.

¤

For twenty-five years and two weeks,
For half of that half century
Which today we celebrate
We have maintained the rage
                                        O let
O let us now,
For this one day
Put aside all dutiful rage,
Suspend payment of accounts and taxes,
Defer even the sorting of things into categories
Each in his office or parlour.
                                        Instead
Let us drink wine
While admiring these afternoon reflections
                                                    And let
This day edged with gold leaf
And fringed with spray
                              rise
Like the shining, marvellous, cusped whale fluke
From the harbour of days.

¤

The Golden Verses of Pythagoras
The Golden Section and the Parthenon,
The Golden Fleece resplendent on its tree,

The Golden Ass and Bowl and Targe and Bough,
The Golden Age still glowing in the dark,
The Golden Hind at anchor — all of these

Recede into a kind of monument
Deflecting sunlight on these golden fields
Saluting this most aureate of days.

And in this grotto where we spread our cloth
This Cloth of Gold for sandwiches and wine
We sense a shadowy presence in the trees.

A ghostly Anderson leans from a cloud:
"I've had my eye on you, my lad. You have
Found several holes in my aesthetics. Yet

It's pleasant over here and I can say
That nothing much has changed as yet. There's still
One way of being, one at most of knowing,

No First Cause, no Absolute of course,
And 'good' is still an attribute like 'green'.
But I digress. I like your style, and so

I'm sending you and your good wife a sign."
The trees look startled, realism glows
And X-rays shimmer in the sea and sky.

¤

In 1950 these were headline news:
The end of wartime petrol rationing;
The Communist Party Dissolution Bill;
John Antill's triumph with *Corroboree*;
Lake Eyre is flooded "for the first time since
The last ice age." (Professor Douglas Mawson);
A cyclone moving down the coast kills seven;
The publication of *A Town Like Alice*;
Rabbit Destruction Authority set up;
The author of *Power Without Glory* charged;
Joan Sutherland wins Australia's Mobil Quest;
The basic wage is raised to £8.6s;
The controversial Harry Seidler builds
His 'International' house at Turramurra;
Sir Arthur Fadden says Australia
Is "on the brink of great prosperity";
Last issue of *Smiths Weekly* on the stands;
The hit song of the year is *Mona Lisa*.

¤

Max Meldrum, Tonal Painter,
Another Scot, takes up this fractive torch.
Diminutive and similarly moustached,
He cries, "Congratulations on this day

To you, O painter-bride of fifty years
And loyal keeper of the faith. Note how
The silver harbour with its gilded shore

Waxes and wanes as tone flows over tone.
I always knew that I was right! Your work
Has been a comfort to me over here

Where paint is pigment-free but light's too bright.
But just as in your painting you've excelled,
I praise the way you've held the tinted glass

Of wisdom, humour and restraint, to calm
The highly coloured incandescent glare
Of William's mind." And now these pale wraiths fade.

The seagulls rise and circle and return
To rise and fall again buoyed in the swell
Across the wedding band of harbour gold.

¤

When will you marry me Ethel
He uttered. You must be my wife
It has come to that I love you
So intensely that if you say no
I shall perforce dash my body
To the brink of yon muddy river
He panted wildly. Oh don't do that
Implored Ethel breathing rather hard
Then say you love me he cried
Oh Bernard she sighed fervently
I certainly love you madly You are
To me like a Heathen god she cried
Looking at his manly form and handsome
Flashing face I will indeed marry you.

¤

A Family Album

A flat in Kings Cross. Edna. Dot.
A sudden storm at Bondi Beach
When hail rained down like jagged fruit.
Amorous lightning soon would strike
      And in its fork what alchemy!

The Court Reporter in his suit
Proceeds to library catalogues
At Parliament. He serves the State.
Prufrockian gas ring boiling eggs.
      Soon earth will yield its reef of gold:

The vital link is Eric Shaw
Who Bore the Rod in Parliament.
Through him they meet. And evermore
The quickening heart and pulse. And soon
      White veils. O my America!

The Murray river's olive shoals
And tree-lined banks by rowing boat.
And after library index files
(While Ewan toddles on the beach)
      Late sunlight in a Bondi tram.

Taringa, Brisbane. Home Sweet Home:
At hilly, dead-end Howitt Street
The long night of the curtain hem,
Repairs to cisterns, fittings, drains.
      Three children under six to draw.

With Mr Potts from Real Estate:
The sunlight washed through trees and glass
Flooding 11 Hercules Street
And afternoon flowed down the hall
      To lay down seams of future gold.

Here dinner parties, Christmas plays,
Admiring students, guinea-pigs,
Mitzi the corgi, crowded days.
And piles of books begat more books
      For travel in the realms of gold.

A tent at Hat Head summer long
And Marcia walking in the waves,
Mitzi and Penny following.
At sunset, on the waves, a kind
      Of Golden Road to Samarkand.

The Fairsea. Fumes of diesel oil.
Rum cakes and lamb's brains to sustain
The Blackfriars Correspondence School.
Jim's measles threaten quarantine.
      And Neptune's trumpet blazoning.

4, All Saints' Close in Chigwell Row.
The British library. Galleries.
The milk truck and the church hedge. Glow
Of Courtauld Institute Cezannes —
      All laying down prolific gold.

Trig's Tales of Darkest India:
Coffee and biscuits (Do Not Dunk).
A welcoming vase of Wandering Jew.
A painting class at Willoughby,
            Jim Sharp in Meldrum's muted light.

From Craven A to fragrant pipe
And yellow tins of Erinmore.
And nightly, while four children sleep,
The kitchen is a web of words,
            Proper words in proper places.

Two more sabbaticals. The first
At 34 Kings Hall Road, Penge
(Another Bedford — blue); the last
At Corkscrew Hill, West Wickham. Words
            Again rise through the fumes of paint.

Jasmine, the German Shepherd Cross,
Now comes from Sutherland to live,
A friend to all grandchildren, less
To members of the world at large.
            Still grain on grain of river gold —

As teacher, William has excelled
And Marcia, teacher of good cheer.
Each has laid down such seams of gold
That, with Defoe, all cry, We loved
            The doctrine for the teacher's sake.

MITTENTIS VOTA SECVNDAT

For William Maidment in
His Convalescence

To use language so that it resonates
Like a bell underwater, volubly
And powerfully or merrily, as it does
In Coral Browne's reply in the following,
Is the aim of every practitioner
In the arts of manufacturing lip glosses:
The Australian actress latterly well known
In her role as Mrs Vincent Price
Was running for a taxi which she reached
Fractionally ahead of an unknown man
To whom the driver said, "I think,
Sir, this lady beat you to it."
He demanded with his head inside
The taxi door, "Which lady?"
And Coral Browne at the other door
Said loudly, "This fucking lady."
The name Coral Browne sounds comfortably
Antipodean as would perhaps Wattle
Smith or Waratah Higgins or even
Echidna Simpson (after the desert)
Or Boronia Jones. And the quality
Of provincial incisiveness appears
Again in a second Coral Browne story:
Telephoning for seats at Charlton Heston's
Shaky *Macbeth*, a production said to leave
Much to be desired, she said, "Coral Browne
Wishes to reserve two seats for tonight's
Performance." The girl was haughty. The house
Was full. Coral Browne said, "Young lady,
This is Mrs Vincent Price, could you arrange...?"
Still no seats could be found and still
The girl was haughty. Next, Coral Browne said,
"All right. Then I'll have two seats

For the second half." Such
Lapidary acerbity is shared
By Maggie Smith's languid "Aren't we all?",
Spoken on seeing the author
Of the play in which she was acting
Standing in the wings. On asking
Why he looked darkly disturbed
He had replied, "I am having
Trouble with my new play."
One might adduce here too the indefatigable
Mrs Siddons, née Kemble, tragedienne,
Who in retirement maintained the tragic
In the involuntary blank verse of command
In addressing domestics. Thus,
"You've brought me water, boy; I asked for beer"
And "Beef cannot be too salt for me, my lord."
To the person convalescing, may this
General and variegated effluvium
Have the celebrated curative power
Of sustained doses of Vitamin C
In the best possible case scenario
As envisaged by Linus Pauling.
Thus far the prologue: from which has been
Excised some measure of irrelevance as may
Have been dragged in by a recital,
For example, of Little Known Knock Knocks
From Shakespeare, such as "Knock knock."
"Who's there?" "Mandy." "Mandy Who?"
"Man delights not me; no, nor woman neither",
And even poorer instances involving
Leon Macduff, and so on. And may
These effusions and efflorescences carry forward
A levelling of the fever-chart

With the restorative charm of concentrated garlic,
So that in recital words take on
The power of wide spectrum anti-toxins.
Thus the prologue. Soon an incident
(As incidents, hovering between
Impulse and stasis, frequently do)
Now supervenes: A man (let us
With leaping arbitrariness name him
Trefusis) steps on to the viewing platform
Above the railway cutting just as
The crane towering over the valley
Above the un-Copernican sun scarcely
Risen from the shadowy quarry moves
And drops a plinth of granite
To scatter like wattle pollen
Narrowly missing a passing convoy
Of wedding cars amongst which
A taxi is being approached on two fronts.
A breeze reversing the poplar leaves
Makes moonlight of sunlight.
Smoothing his hair Trefusis addresses
His exquisitely swathed companion:
"As well you know, and have remarked,
I am curious about the origins of things,
Or, rather, of certain curious terms,
For instance, 'horse latitudes'... Is this not
Quite as poetic as 'salad days'
And other delights Shakespearian?"
Later, as they sit nearby
For coffee and iced sweetbreads
Under a calm beige umbrella
Overlooking the construction zone
He smiles as he opens a newspaper,

Almost at random, and reads, "A man
Was found wandering dazed today in a henhouse
At Wilton. Police called to the scene suspect
Foul play." To the recuperant
One might offer this light-hearted
Sunlit transparency of solecism
As a model of the pleasures
To be found on his return to the shores
Of the high-altitude lake of well-being
Having triumphed over a snaggle of viruses
Or a bacterium as large as itself
Magnified under a microscope.
And if delight in facts can be seen
As a measure of such a triumph,
Might not optimism suggest
The reversal of this transaction, viz
The therapeutic use of facts as anti-biotic?
Accordingly, a book flies gracefully down
Floating and flying like the pelican
Whose bones are light and filled with air
Floating on the air over the water.
It falls on to the viewing platform,
Open at a page which, by a chance
As long as life itself, contains
The following beguiling information:
— Horse latitudes are sub-tropical bands
Of high atmospheric pressure over the oceans
Between the Trade Winds and the Westerlies.
They move north and south with the sun.
They are regions of calms, and winds
Light to variable, of dry air and quiet,
Stable conditions, the sort of weather
One associates with horses grazing

On the ocean of a generous paddock,
To say nothing of the connection of horses
With stables. Some say
Dog-days tend to happen frequently
In horse latitudes. The term may
Refer also to the casting adrift
Of horses on a glassy sea from ships
Becalmed en route to the Indies.
The breeze turned several pages:
Meanders tend to increase in curvature
By erosion and aggregation until
Eventually one will form a loop.
A naze is a promontory or headland.
Mud-rain, when the dust is red
Is sometimes known as blood-rain.
A muskeg is a swamp filled
With sphagnum moss in tundra.
Calving is the detachment
Of an iceberg from a glacier;
There seems scope here for the development
Of alternative terms of venery.
Oozes are classified as calcareous
Or siliceous and are named in accordance
With the creatures which on the sea-plain
Inhabit them; thus, Pteropod Ooze,
Radiolanian Ooze, Globigerina Ooze.
An iceblink is a white glare
Arched over the horizon and caused
By reflection from a mass of ice
Which is itself too distant to be visible.
A wind rose is a diagram in which
Prevailing winds array themselves.
A ubac is a mountain slope

Perpetually shaded from the sun's rays
Like a sheet of paper being read;
In Italy it is called opaco
In whose shadow we may discern
Snow glimmerings of the word 'opacity'.
A Vardarac is a cold wind
Which blows from the mountains, and shares
Many of the characteristics of the mistral.
The tropopause is a boundary layer
Between troposphere and stratosphere. Here
At a height of five to ten miles
Above the earth's enamelled surface
Tea could not be brewed since water boils
Too readily at such low pressures;
But a compensation for the intrepid
Would be the splendid views.
The rainbow celebrates division;
The secondary rainbow is a reflection
Of the primary bow and thus
Has its colours in reverse order.
A fogbow is white and is seen
Opposite the sun in dense fog;
It is a rainbow which is white
Because its scales of colour overlap.
A fluvioglacial is a glaciofluvial.
Drift-ice is self-explanatory.
A poem is a caldera in that
A caldera is a lake formed
By the subsidence of a volcano.

Entropy

In the Eighteenth Century, de Mairan discovered
The biological clock in several heliotrope plants
Which even when confined in total darkness
Opened themselves by day and closed at night.
Even more significantly, human volunteers, deprived
Of all indicators of time for a hundred days
Were found to go to sleep an hour later every day,
Which suggests that humans have a twenty-five hour clock.
This phenomenon of drift is called 'free-riding'.
Aware that verses expressing sympathy
For one in some stage of depletion who is
Feeling out of sorts, below par, poorly,
Seedy, peaky, peevish or not himself
(Or all or any of the above) must revive
Echoes of that more famous bulletin
'He is no better. He is just the same',
I remark nonetheless that you in your own struggle
With entropy (which shall shortly be defined)
Must inhabit a world somewhat akin to that
Of these sleep subjects. They of course
Were deprived of all evidence from which they might
Deduce the time of day. Laboratory officers
Were at all times to avoid five-o'clock shadows.
Newspapers or magazines were always a few days
Out of date. Meals were not necessarily
Classifiable as 'breakfast'or 'lunch' or 'dinner'.
Rosters for monitoring staff were randomly
Rotated, and in the hearing of subjects they were
To avoid references to what they did 'last night'.
Entropy increases. It is a measure
Of the amount of disorder in a system — witness
The child's refutation of the proposition 'Nothing is impossible',
'Ever try putting the toothpaste back in the tube?'

Drifting is a way of representing entropy,
A place for everything and few things in their places.
The convalescent listlessly turning away
From the morning newspaper and, weakly voicing
Distaste at its dross, is a testimony to entropy.
The tendency for entropy to increase poses problems
For cosmologists, positing as it does the question:
If everything is running downhill always,
Why don't the sun and stars in festive fusion
And the constellations in their cosmic dance
Simply give up, slow down, drift
And pull the covers over their heads and refuse
To get up to face the indifferent weather of time?
And in the domestic arena (in whose grandstand you sit
Rugged up in overcoat and muffler) we are constantly
Made aware of the energy losses in systems
Implicit in the Second Law of Thermodynamics;
For example, from the *Women's Weekly* the following
Amusing instance of Longitudinal Thinking,
"My husband having lost the bottom button
From his cardigan said, 'Don't you worry.
I can sew on a button.' But when,
More than an hour later he had failed
To reappear I grew curious and went
Into the sewing room. There he was still
Laboriously and irritably completing the job
Of moving each button down one place."
But now to the principal purpose of this dissertation
Medicinal (which is to be taken with the usual
Grain of salt) viz. to distract and delay
The onset of that rising tide of entropy
Which threatens to engulf us all
By the hasty adducement of delights, entertainments

Or at least novelties which may engage
Beguile or dandle the patient in his infirmary.
My first impulse: to command a flummery
Of confections, a collation of Street Cries, viz:
Strawberries, green pease, lobsters, non pareils,
Curds and whey, hot saloop, sparrowgrass, cherries.
Until I remember the delicate condition
In which you languish and repine with drawn shades,
And I recall the faculty of gustatory suggestion
(Together with adjacent dictionary entries gut, gutsy, gustful)
Whose existence is evidenced by a brief passage
From the *Pen and Ink Sketches of Poets, Preachers and Politicians*
By John Ross Dix (1846) [Fisher Library, never borrowed.]
Coleridge is seen 'fixed in reverie' 'trying to guess
The whereabouts of his little dusky room
Behind the warehouse. Ah! he smells in the fine frenzy
Of *gastric imagination* the soup.' (my emphases.)
A page further on John Dix gives incidentally
An instance of entropy averted. Coleridge
Has referred to his 'fortunate reclamation
From a rage for metaphysical disputation
That threatened utterly to engross his entire mind.'
So, to avoid all risk of ruminative rumble
I veer hastily from the culinary to the following,
Itself a fine example of increasing entropy
As the would-be recipients of charity dissolve into yelps
Of fugitive alarm. It is Walpole's account
Of Henry James about to present a few coins
To some worthy country urchins. He holds out the coppers
But first cautions them: they were to go
To a certain sweet shop because there the sweets
Were better than any other; they were to see
That they were not deceived and offered an inferior brand,

For those particular sweets had a peculiar taste of nuts
And honey with, he fancied, an especial flavour
That was almost the molasses of his own country.
If the children took care to visit the right shop
And insisted that they should have only
That particular sweet called, he fancied, "Honey Nut"
— Or was it something with "delight" in it? "Rye's Delight"
Or "Honey Delights" — But at that moment the children
Who had been listening open-mouthed, their eyes fixed
On the pennies, of a sudden took fright and turned
Running and roaring with terror across the field.
He stood bewildered, the pennies in his hand. What
Had he done? What had he said? He had meant
Nothing but kindness. Why had they run from him
Crying and screaming? He was greatly distressed, going over
Every possible corner of it in his mind.
He alluded to it for days afterwards.
Distress and confusion, possible concomitants of entropy,
May alternate with disillusion or disapproval
As in the following perplexing exchange:
On a wall covered with graffiti someone had remarked
'Everything written here is exceptionally uninteresting.'
To which someone had added the reply
'Since they are many they cannot be exceptional.'
I cannot decide if this is valid. Certainly
The second statement is interesting, and this adds
A frisson of reflexive paradox to the first.
Of course, the assumption implicit so far, that entropy
Is no good thing, must be resisted.
The relaxation principle, the irreversibility of much change,
And indeed the minor ailment imposing an unexpected
View of the yard through the wooden slats
From the menthol sheets of the fever room —

These may be beneficent, genial and restorative.
The patient after a time rises refreshed
To find westerly winds have swept a modicum
Of pollution out to sea leaving the city skyline
Confidingly luminous. This may be as salutary
As a change of latitude or swimming in late autumn.
Everything being relative, a principle of relativity,
That a warm day in winter is worth any number
Elsewhere, for example, may well be the only absolute
Which we can extract after a lifetime of panning
In the oblivious, unhelpful and glistening river.
But aspects of faltering, my true subject, eventually
Turn on themselves. Questions are asked in the house
Of cards, notably: in the pursuit of the variegate
(The quartz aggregate spangled with points of gold)
Can diversity distinguish itself from the merely arbitrary?
By now the recuperant holding wanly this heavy sheaf
May well have reached for laudanum
And with brow suddenly registering an increase in fever
Have fallen back on his pillow, letting these leaves
Flutter to the floor, while outside the light
Passes an implicit judgement on the dangers of excess.
Nevertheless one would like to ask succinctly:
In an aesthetic based on surprise and disjunction
What would disbar any particular item from inclusion?
If the symphony "should contain the whole world", raising
The *ad hoc* to the status of the *sine qua non*
While stopping short, one hopes of the *ad nauseam*,
It is ironical that the Goldberg Variations, commissioned
To cure insomnia, are in fact so rivettingly long.
'I was charmed,' writes John Dix of Coleridge,
'With the vague splendours of his thought, coruscating
Like a boreal aurora but I confess the matter of fact

That gave rise to them seemed indeed veiled by them
— Veiled by "excess of light"; the matter where this glory
Or halo of language was to impress upon the mind
Remained somewhat in the state of the earthly movements
— Wars, battles, sieges — prefigured by that heavenly
Northern illumination. It was too like the state produced,
According to Dr Johnson, by the gorgeous poetry of Akenside
"Sometimes amazed, always delighted, it recollected little
And carried away nothing."' This is precisely
(If that is the word) the danger in these speculative saline drips,
That eventually manner overtakes matter, and exhausts
(In an image of the reader as a prostrate Chatterton
An arm faintly resting across the counterpane)
Even the most avid or dedicated quidnunc:
From Latin *quid* what plus *nunc* now: one who is
Constantly asking 'What now?' hence an inquisitive person.
1709, Steele, Tatler No. 10: 'The insignificancy of my Manners
Makes the laughers call me a Quid Nunc.'
1782, Cowper: '... no small figure amongst the Quidnuncs of Olney.'
1804, in Spirit Pub Jrnls VIII 93, 'His attachment
To quidnunckery is as constant as ever.'
But alas, even the most ardent quidnunc
Must weary of quiddling in the pursuit of quiddities
And the relentlessly frequent *quid pro quo*,
And prefer instead a liberal serving
Of quiddany (a thick fruit soup or jelly,
Originally made from quinces) or may at last long
For quiescence and quiet if not quietus.

Memorial

To interpose the figure of Prince Tomasi di Lampedusa in the void left by the departure of William Maidment should seem no more arbitrary than might be thought Cruel Fortune which enforced this loss.

In these days of loss like a warm ever-present breeze, there is the consolation of transcribing something long-loved and, in the process, testing the possibilities and limits of modulation.

Lampedusa:

"First of all our home. I loved it with utter abandon and still love it now when for the last twelve years it has been no more than a memory."

"Until a few months before its destruction I used to sleep in the room where I was born, five yards away from the spot where my mother's bed had stood when she gave me birth."

"So it will be very painful for me to evoke my dead Beloved as she was until 1929 in her integrity and beauty and as she continued after all to be until 5th April 1943, the day on which bombs brought from beyond the Atlantic searched her out and destroyed her."

Uncanny resemblance to a canny reader of semblances:

This impulse to transcription began two weeks ago. At the Department of English, a white-haired man stepped out, bearing an impossible resemblance to W.M. – impossible since W.M. has left us. He conveyed Bill's distraction-by-thought and long-familiar gravity. He even carried a haversack of books and persisted for a radiance, long enough to suggest in that wild surmise the reversal of all grief.

This resonant sighting, this chance resemblance, oddly mimicked the frequent chance meetings I had enjoyed with Bill in halcyon days as he crossed the quadrangle or approached the library with his haversack of books.

And at his house where one passed down corridors of books with doors opening on rooms of books, he sat on the wide beach of a leather lounge, *a reader at bay*.

Reading is translation and, insofar as he was reading for much of his life, Bill resembled Lampedusa who visited the same patisserie every morning for breakfast and to read; Lampedusa translating memory and loss into *Places of My Infancy*, Archibald Colquhoun translating this memoir into English with its cautionary "I can promise to say nothing that is untrue but do not think I shall want to say all; and I reserve the right to lie by omission."

And these *Places of My Infancy* – childhood and childhood's houses all irretrievably gone – take on the template of *our* loss. And one other who is as affected by his – Bill's – absence as I, contemplates the unmelting glacier of bereavement; he swims; he reads; he suffers; he constructs cascades of words more glittering, more salmon-leaping, more suddenly dividing between rocks, more foaming, more hung with mist than mine*. But we each follow the rapids towards that absence.

"It was the Princess who originally to calm her husband's nostalgia first encouraged him to write…" (Colquhoun). This sentence itself fills me with its own nostalgia, and suggests now our own overwhelming nostalgia at this absence.

Lampedusa's loss – of the architecture of childhood – was the result of American bombing. To us in the case of W.M. there was no explosion, no sound, no shattered Murano glass, no debris.

The order imposed by the formalising power of *statement* ensures that it is impossible to set down grief, which is essentially disorder. Even in the case of the Palermo bombing what remains with the rubble is nostalgia and perhaps a form of vehemence or sadness, but the loss, being irreparable, is largely inexpressible.

Often, to voice these matters, we find ourselves equipped with little more than windchimes or Aeolian harp as our only instruments of expression.

In the patisserie over breakfast or at café tables at lunch, Lampedusa wrote *Il Gattopardo*. The novel appeared after his death. Final revisions were not possible.

---

* See David Musgrave: *Anatomy of Voice*, The Third Partition.

An article in The Yale Review (LXXXIX No. 2) details some sonnets written by Don Fabrizio (the hero of that novel) and a few lyrics by his nephew Tancredi, intended for *Il Gattopardo* but never included.

Two research library citations: under the rubric *Lampedusa,*
1) *Marine grottoes on the island of Lampedusa;*
2) *Decapod crustaceans of the trawlable sea bed around the island of Lampedusa.*

After the death of his father, possession of this island of amber sand and diving caves passed to the author of *The Leopard* and *Places of My Infancy*. The island has become a further emblem of loss in becoming the destination of endangered refugees.

Navigation is hazardous between the island and the mainland because the sea is shallow. This fact too offers itself as an emblem.

William Maidment, whose sudden departure *from the library of countless pages* has so affected us, is celebrated through these shards, which lie like the rubble still spread over the Via Lampedusa since the American bombings a lifetime ago.

In the library I pass in the vaults many earnest researchers; but none has the incisive calm, the Swiftian irony, the passionate bemusement to be noted in Bill's *questing* or *questioning*: *Only connect / everything with everything*

Excursion:
We were to travel by small underpowered ferry to an island in the Hawkesbury / calling first at an escarpment settlement popularly known as Falling Rock / since it is so steep as to seem to threaten houses below it. / The ferry sat low in the water and was accompanied by the twin wasp wings of wake / beginning near the prow. W.M. seemed to relish everything, the little chromed chain / linked as a token protection across the open doorway onto the water, / the drifts of grass and weed passing, the occasional plop of a fishjump; / and when we reached the escarpment he was as bemused as I / by the woman who got off

with shopping from the mainland and who mounted half a dozen steps / to her house and, while we still idled, boiled an electric kettle and made tea. / All this while the chain still swung loose and the motor waited for some other signal to reverse. / Then the wasp wings of white wake resumed. The motor sounded. Pelicans flew on towards the island /and a channel of corrugated water intervened. I noted again in the white-haired companion of my late late adolescence / the smile of reason. A dog was waiting on the island jetty. There was a hill / to the west with cliffs. In the south we descended / to a beach which seemed not to shelve. The river was more like a lake. / Ropes anchored on the grass above the beach ran in lines out into the shallow water and disappeared. / To the east there were flowering trees. Circumambulation led us past oysters and mud and reinforcing timbers / and a few narrow jetties with signs warning against trespass. / To reach the jetty again required crossing private property—the mute buffalo lawns / mown only at weekends with their houses boarded up or empty. / A certain desolation now attaches to such places.

The sense of loss, still palpable, seems nonetheless attenuated—as thin and pervasive as the air.

In the Taviani brothers' film *Kaos* there is an affecting coda in which Pirandello travels to a deserted railway station and thence by cart to his former home. Here his mother, now a memory, engages him in a confusion of memories; the one he seeks is that of the sailing excursion to the pumice islands. The children are allowed to bathe while their mother sits under a parasol. They clamber up the pumice slopes and run down them into the water. This memory too is saturated or dense with the sense of loss made the more persuasive by the cadential music and the faded colour of pumice and the Tyrrhenian or similar much-used sea.

Towards A Convergence

L: "Those seas used continuously since the days of Homer"

And texts read continuously for as long.

L: "The avenue was really grandiose; about three hundred yards long, it went straight towards the top of the hill, bordered on each side by a double row of cypresses, not adolescent cypresses like those of St Guido but great trees almost a hundred years old whose thick branches spread in every season their austere scent."

In that Void a Tendency to Vain Elaboration

The avenue was long and grandiose
And climbed for some three hundred yards towards
The hill crest bordered all along its length
By cypresses in double rows—and not,
As at St Guido's, adolescent groves—
But trees established for a hundred years
Whose heavy branches, independently
Of season, spread abroad their austere scent.

L: "Another of the oddities of the house was the table-centre in the dining room. This was a large fixed silver ornament, surmounted by Neptune who threatened the guests with his trident, while beside him an Amphitrite eyed them with a hint of malice. The whole was set on a rock rising in the middle of a silver basin, surrounded by dolphins and marine monsters squirting water from their mouths through some machinery hidden in a central part of the table. It was all very gay and grand but had the inconvenience of requiring tablecloths with a large hole cut out of the middle for Neptune."

Donnafugata: "The house of Santa Margherita was a kind of eighteenth century Pompeii preserved miraculously—rare enough in any case but here in Sicily so given to neglect and poverty almost unique—"

"I do not know what were the causes of this durability—perhaps the fact that my maternal grandfather endured a kind of exile there for twenty years imposed on him by several Bourbon Kings resulting from a misdemeanour on the Grand Marine Parade at Palermo."

Lampedusa supplies a footnote: "Driving out stark naked in his carriage"

Increasing Turbulence of the Wake

The choice of Giuseppe Tomasi di Lampedusa
as a surrogate presence for Bill Maidment ensures
that he will take on our sorrows, in that

First, he embodies the deep nostalgia that we feel
in looking back over this disturbed wake;
 second he embodies in the extreme the archetype of *reader*.

In Palermo he visited Flaccovio the bookseller
"every day for ten years". Tolstoy, Stendhal, Proust;
Flaubert, Dickens engaged him profoundly.

Every morning he walked to the patisserie
where he breakfasted and read. Once he did not move
from his table for four hours during which time

He read an entire novel by Balzac. His bag of books
was always excessive. Together with cakes held over
from breakfast he always carried copies of Proust

And Shakespeare; the latter in his wife's view
in case he needed to console himself
"should he encounter some unpleasantness".

Bill's house, an inexhaustible and exhaustive library, and his
crowded locker in the university library in the little alcove where
someone had written on the wall above it *The horror, the horror!*
—were a similar testament to the single-minded or Puritanical
excesses of his reading.

This Grave Loss Which Does not Diminish

The novels of Smollett, Richardson, Fielding
 In each of us the loss was palpable.
Fresh strawberries taken with black tea
 How differently it manifests itself
A vast collection of minor statuary from charity shops
 According to sporadic memories
Emblem books embodying the most arcane virtues
 Or accidents of contiguity
A remarkably iconographic sensibility
 Or chance encounters in the public square.
The capacity to see symbols in every configuration
 In each of us the loss has long endured
Delight in the simplest rendering of a landscape
 And yet these sadnesses grow similar
Rowing down the Murray from Swan Hill
 As when beguiled by false resemblances
Revisiting the diffuse memories of the Hunter
 We each turn half elated in the street
At Bondi Beach the confiding of the final illness
 Only to fall again into regret.

L: "Everything about the house I loved:
The strange irregularities of its walls,
The excessive number of its drawing-rooms,
The ceiling stucco's labyrinthine maze,
The smells of spices from the kitchen doors,
The scent of violets in the mirrored air
So constant in my mother's dressing room,
The stables' stuffiness, the ancient cool
Of polished leather in the saddle room,
The mystery of the apartments still unfinished
On the upper floors, the coach house mute
With carriages, a world entirely filled
With sweet surprises and great mysteries
Repeatedly, perpetually renewed."

We who regret the many metonymies
Which mark real pain,
We who see the earth's rotation round the sun
And its ancillary idling on its axis
As achieving no closure,
We whose days now pass without mentor ...

In the case of Lampedusa at his café table for years, private language eventually becomes public and, after his death, emerges as *The Leopard*.

Private languages, that old chestnut, now showing in a brazier near you!

Individual grief a source of private language!

A recent arrival amongst spring conifers, the North American robin sings and proposes some of the requirements of language: variation, consistency over a range, close or apparent repetition, pauses, emphases, animated afterthoughts. The butcher-bird however suggests something wordless, closer to scat singing; delight or reverie or celebration as distinct from articulation of argument and *statement*.

And the wild geese their klaxon? That too sounds very like language.

In the private landscape of bereavement, we mourners walk. By the sea, on the river bank, *lost in thought*, we pass the very place where he walked – under sparrow cries, by gorse hedge and trailing bindweed, beside the river carrying grass islands downstream.

Lampedusa disliked melodrama and Italian opera. He suffered from insomnia and nightmares.

The vividness of poetry emerging in physical detail – as in the oranges that follow. L: "the mermaid sighted off the Sandwich Islands in March 1869 was seen, when the sailors threw her oranges, to have a magnificent range of yellowed teeth."

Lampedusa's siren in the exemplary story *Lighea* had white, sharp-pointed teeth.

Lampedusa thought Sonnet 129 – "Th'expense of spirit ..." – the greatest of the 40 or so he considered masterpieces; his favourite play was *Measure for Measure*. In this he expresses a passionate scepticism which might suggest W.M.

Bill would perhaps name Milton, Spenser, Swift, Smollett, Joyce, Burke *On The Sublime*, perhaps even Tom Collins: *Such is Life*.

A digression into the endless pages of the monumental, possibly

infinite book, *Oceanic Intimations* or *Cataloguing the Arbitrary*, in
which, like Ulysses, Bill sought deep waters and the sirens:

Turning through the pages at which it falls open
And noting how loss erodes focus
And induces endless enumerations:

A film-still showing Bette Davis in *All About Eve*
standing at the staircase and, behind her,
Reynold's *Sarah Siddons as the Tragic Muse.*

A photograph recording Bette Davis at Laguna Beach,
for one night only, posing in a *tableau vivant*
as Reynold's *Sarah Siddons as the Tragic Muse.*

An illustration for the scene from *Candide*, Ch.16,
in which Candide and Cacambo chance upon
two monkeys biting at two girls' naked bums.

The George du Maurier cartoon *The Six Mark Teapot*
with *Aesthetic Bridegroom* and *Intense Bride*, who holds
the teapot and says, "Oh Algernon Let Us Live Up To It."

A picture of Kelmscott Manor and a late portrait
of Jane Morris looking ten feet tall, shortly before
her discovery of Rossetti's addiction to chloral.

Morris had gone to Iceland. "Let us hope
Tops is up to his navel in ice and likes it"
(letter from Rossetti with Jane Morris in view.)

Rossetti's first large oil of Jane showing a carnation
on an open book "suggesting rhyme",
in particular Leigh Hunt's curious lines,

"One's sighs and passionate declarations
in odorous rhetoric of carnations" (!)
And yet "odorous rhetoric" is good, is it not?

Carlyle, whom Bill admired, characterised fiction
as "more than we suspect of the nature of lying,"
putting this view in the mouth of a fictional character.

A breeze blows the pages open at the face
of Kim Novak in San Francisco, impassive – or, rather,
limning the limits of the expressive.

And a few pages further on under the rubric
One of the supreme representations of representation,
an elaborate deconstruction of Courbet's *Studio*

Whose full title is, with its charming oxymoron,
*The Painter's Studio, Real Allegory, Summing Up
A Phase of Seven Years in My Artistic Life,*

Allegory (implicit in every aspect of W.M.)
is the naked model representing Truth
who watches Courbet paint.

Note also the white cat playing with a ball,
the waterfall in the inner painting partly executed,
and the drapes let fall expressively at the model's feet;

And as an allegory of reading we might remark
the fact that Baudelaire at the extreme right reads
and takes no interest in the studio or its painting.

And Delacroix's consolation on the Academy's rejection:
"A strapping lad like Courbet is not going
to be discouraged by so small a thing as that."

"Courbet in his landscapes sometimes conferred
on rocks and vegetation the appearance
of human faces and animal heads."

Here is mimesis and the paradox, by W.M.
long pondered: that mimesis is seductive
while nonetheless art is not mimesis.

*And yet we have turned through little more than the first few pages of
the book which may well be illimitable.*

Lampedusa drank only water. He smoked heavily. His conversation
was "brilliant and precise, pleasant and slightly sarcastic." He spoke
to his dogs in several languages (and they invariably understood
him).

Example of a line beginning with two reversed feet:
We who suffer this irreversible loss –

"The sirens are to be seen as the traces of past affections which
reverberate across the sea of the present."

A line ending with an unstressed syllable:
We each follow the rapids towards that absence.

We who share this task of grief
And are rowing on its dark Tyrrhenian Sea
Are startled when from time to time
The siren of memory as in Lampedusa's story
Clambers aboard and beguiles us with overwhelming *presence.*

Gryll Grange:
A Synopsis

1

"Palestine soup!' said the Reverend Doctor Opimian, dining with his friend Squire Gryll; 'a curiously complicated misnomer.'" This opening sentence introduces a pleasing disintrication by Doctor Opimian involving an explanation of the confusion of two artichoke species, and slippages in translation. Such unfolding serves as an emblem of the randomness and charm to which every work should aspire. This excellent opening also invites comment about beginnings in general. It is a truth universally acknowledged that the opening sentence should stand like a folly overlooking the surrounding woods and still be visible to the traveller no matter how far he roams. A friend has pointed to the pleasing opening of *The Towers of Trebizon* by Rose Macaulay as a worthy instance: " 'Take my camel, dear,' said my Aunt Dot, as she climbed down from this animal on her return from high mass."

This could be accompanied by the beginning of *Calidore*, an unfinished fragment by the author of *Gryll Grange*: "NOTWITHSTANDING the great improvements of machinery in this rapidly improving age, which is so much wiser, better, and happier than all that went before it, every gentleman is not yet accommodated with the convenience of a pocket boat. We may therefore readily imagine that Miss Ap-Nanny and her sister Ellen, the daughters of the Vicar of Llanglasrhyd, were not a little astonished in a Sunday evening walk on the sea shore, when a little skiff, which, by the rapidity of its motion had attracted their attention while but a speck upon the waves, ran upon the beach, from which emerged a very handsome young gentleman, dressed not exactly in the newest fashion, who, after taking down the sail and hauling up the boat upon the beach, carefully folded it up in the size of a prayer-book and transferred it to his pocket."

Doctor Opimian, not easily discouraged, instances further misnomers by way of disparaging other inequities and abuses in society. The conversation then drifts downstream to the topic of fish, acceptable species of a single syllable and of two and three, with a pleasant disagreement as to the virtues of bream. This leads to mention of the expected arrival of Lord Curryfin, who is touring with his lecture on fish. Miss Gryll, the unmarried niece of Mr Gryll, finds the concept of a lecturing lord comical. Doctor Opimian agrees, insofar as he considers the lecture an inferior form to the debate or, better, the *tenson*, a twelfth-century discussion of love and chivalry. Mr Gryll proposes a further improvement towards an Aristophanic comedy where debate and exposition are amplified by a *Chorus*. Such an enterprise is suggested for Christmas festivities at the Grange, possibly on the topic of *spirit-rapping*, a current craze.

The present pot-pourri or mélange or commentary or compote or carillon of synopses or transcription for hand-bells or riff or walking-tour of Gryll Grange must encounter the rapids of irrelevance; anachronism may sometimes threaten its fabric, indulgence elaborate its hems.

The maker of synopses must always hope that a previous reader (of *Gryll Grange*) or one who has never taken that volume from its shelves will eventually, even if in another life, read or re-read it.

He (the elaborist) is in the habit of singing while playing at the keyboard – Glenn Gould playing Bach comes to mind.

And he hopes that his Commentary will be *botryose* – that is, "bearing flowers in clusters which develop successively from the base upwards"; and may even be read in a *boreen* – that is, "a glade furnished with a seat for the purpose of viewing a vista of shimmering water".

2

Gregory Gryll Esq. of Gryll Grange, landholder, proud uncle, descendant of "the ancient and illustrious Gryllus, who maintained against Ulysses the superior happiness of the life of other animals to that of the life of man", lived a life of contentment, visited regularly by friends for quiet dinners. His sole company at the Grange is his orphan niece and godchild, Morgana, raised by him since infancy. Her recent rejection of a numerous cavalcade of suitors has made her uncle nervous that the ancient name of Gryll, surviving since the time of Circe, might disappear in the nineteenth century.

A trivial and scarcely plausible jest attaches itself – anachronistically – to the name Gryll: a shuttlecock has sailed through an open window and alighted on a wall. On the wall is the graffito, "I love grils". Under this has been written "It's girls, stupid" and under this again the plaintive "What about us grils?".

On his frequent visits the Reverend Doctor Opimian is likely to discuss with Mr Gryll the notion of transcription and particularly (and anachronistically) the Liszt transcriptions of the Beethoven symphonies. They tend to agree that the transcription for keyboard stresses structure over colour, the form being clearly more sublime. "And how much more difficult and splendid," muses the doctor, "might be a reduction for fortepiano of the *Missa Solemnis*, which I say again renders most of our speculation, inventions and contrivances mere leaves in a gale?"

<h2 style="text-align:center">3</h2>

One summer morning Doctor Opimian, "an athlete in pedestrianism", sets out to walk through the woods to the Folly, a tower several hours distant, which he has heard described but never seen.

On arriving he meets its owner, Mr Algernon Falconer, a stranger who rapidly becomes friend and host. Their meeting is no doubt facilitated by Homer; for a curl of smoke rising from the tower suggests lines relating to Circe's dwelling which the doctor murmurs aloud in the young man's hearing. This accomplished bachelor has purchased with an inheritance the Folly, extended it generously and in the original tower made a bedroom, a dining-room and a library. In the last, on the upper floor, Doctor Opimian is impressed to find an excellent collection of the major works of Latin and Greek, together with numerous works in English, French and Italian. Mr Falconer endorses Porson's remark that "Life is too short to learn German".

Porson, it could be added, was self-taught, a polymath and Greek scholar, who grew up with few books, notable amongst which was one stray volume of Caxton's Cyclopedia washed ashore like Steerforth from a wrecked freighter.

And were we to retraverse the wild woods in search of the doctor still on his way from the vicarage to the tower we might note the intense complexity, the folded inkblot or lace tracery of the woods, as depicted by Samuel Palmer – the tangle of vine or liana round tree trunks as if they were not self-supporting alone, the ink-black pattern of leaves – all eager to be part of the project, Everything An Emblem.

There might even be a schematic but incomplete lime-rick leaning fragrantly in a glade in those woods:

On a midsummer morning …
The doctor sets out ……..
….. without bound
With his Newfoundland hound
On the dew-covered ………

Delighted in the labyrinth, the doctor is pleased to find a fair imitation of one in Mr Falconer's library.

The doctor is invited to refreshment before setting out to return. Mr Falconer explains that he lives alone happily with only female domestics, principal among whom are Seven Sisters. Two of these – girls of about sixteen or seventeen, modestly but prettily dressed, serve hock and madeira and a pleasing selection of cold meats. Afterwards Mr Falconer accompanies him for the part of the way back through the woods.

> I've no doubt had I not been reciting
> Several lines from the Odyssey's flighting
>   It well may have been
>   I might not have been seen
> And life would be much less exciting.

The lime-rick seems ideally suited to the path through the woods.

> Mr Falconer's knowledge of Homer
> Has ensured that I stay no mere dreamer,
>   For within these stone walls
>   His Odyssean halls
> Make the guest his own Vasco da Gama.

4

The Reverend Doctor Opimian and Mr Falconer traverse the forest in the reverse direction towards the vicarage. They discuss the moral opprobrium with which the indiscriminate world might view Mr Falconer's domestic arrangements – that he lives unattached in a household attended by seven maidens, his Vestals, Seven Sisters of whom the Doctor had seen but two and pronounced them pretty. Mr Falconer cheerfully dismisses such lack of charity, and he enthuses over the attractions of living like a hermit at the top of a tower. The doctor notes the charm of forest scenery, whose poignancy the two agree is increased by the likelihood of its destruction under some Act of Enclosure.

An oak with a deer in its shade
Dims the blaze of the foxglove in plaid
　　With the ferns in a frieze
　　Curling up through the breeze
To a beech-grove in beams lightly frayed.

The doctor's marked tendency to meandering speculation and association might be likened to the often remarked preference in Schubert to favour modulation for its own sake, and for lingering in remote keys to suggest distant vistas. Doctor Opimian walked on alone, enjoying, as the faintly familiar landscape passed in reverse, the reverie of thoughts neither advancing nor retreating.

The tower, an excellent library,
A bedroom which he did not see,
The waiting-maids like sunlit shade
That glimmers in a forest glade
Their hair under no Vestal cloud
Such as their Counterparts employed
– Or were true Vestals shaved on entry?

His thoughts now bear upon the question of feminine beauty insofar as it depends on the hair, thoughts running – flowing in the breeze – round him.

Apuleius singles out the head
Denuded of its hair and thus despoiled
Even if descended from the clouds,
Born of the sea and raised amongst its waves ...
Venus herself with her attending Graces,
Cinctured with fragrance, caparisoned in light,
Would still not please the gods nor man
Without her Botticellian plait.

But what of these maidens attending the Tower, with *their* hair unusually luxuriant? He fears that Mrs Opimian would join the world in finding no virtue in their situation.

5

The doctor honouring his promise to return to the Folly set out some days later in midmorning – since he intended to stay overnight. The day was hot; he paused often under trees, noting species which even to him seemed unfamiliar. In the cool of the evening the two friends dined. Doctor Opimian was surprised to see musical instruments set out and even more so to be given a concert by the Seven Sisters dressed in white and purple – the seven Pleiads! After sacred works by Mozart and Beethoven the concert ended with a hymn to Saint Catharine.

Its last line lingered with the doctor and returned even after a pleasant sleep – the Latin text, which might be rendered in the most exquisite and evocative tetrameter, depending as it does on the opening of the flower to its full three syllables: *vi-o-let.*

Seven Pleiads arrayed in white lawn
With their hair piled like clouds before dawn,
    A harp and an organ
    No sign of a Gorgon –
Only glances as soft as a faun.

6

After breakfast Mr Falconer again accompanied his new friend for part of the way back through the forest. They discussed a variant of the Language of Flowers and Mr Falconer was dazzling on the theme. The Codification of the Language of Trees in which he adumbrated the voices, pleas, vociferations, innuendoes, intimations, implications and opinions of many species noted along the way.

Once alone the doctor enjoys the reverie of walking.

> Alone walking home through the woods
> He mused on their lapidary shades
>   But hearing a cry
>   And a heart-rending sigh
> He found a poor swain in the reeds.

The young man is, it transpires after much tactful inquisition, a rejected suitor of one of the Seven Sisters. Harry Hedgerow (for that is his name) is of good yeoman stock but has made no progress, and suffers.

"And what is her name?" said the doctor.

"Dorothy," said the other; "her name is Dorothy. Their names follow, like ABC, only that A comes last. Betsey, Catherine, Dorothy, Eleanor, Fanny, Grace, Anna. But they told me it was not the alphabet they were christened from; it was the key of A minor, if you know what that means."

"I think I do," said the doctor, laughing. "They were christened from the Greek diatonic scale, and make up two conjunct tetrachords, if you know what that means."

The doctor counsels optimism and at the same time sees a ray of hope. He has conceived the idea of introducing Algernon Falconer and Miss Gryll, and he sees that while the Seven Sisters form a sort of obstacle or shield, the marriage of one of them—Dorothy—to Harry Hedgerow would "break the combination".

7

On the number 7, a review: 7 sisters;
7 Vestals (except that these used to be 6);
7 Pleiads; 7 planets (but now more).

Mrs Opimian: 7 Deadly Sins?

The doctor and Mrs Opimian have a spirited conversation on modern follies.

8

In which Lord Curryfin and his lecture on fish are mentioned; plans for the Aristophanic comedy discussed; the suggestion made that Mr Falconer be invited to the Grange in the hope that he will participate; the absurdities of the newfangled Science of Pantopragmatics of which Lord Curryfin's lectures on fish are instanced, being as useless as a cook lecturing on bubble-and-squeak.

And were Doctor Opimian to extend the range of his disparagements into the future, he might well censure that aspect of progress by which the television screen became rectangular and by an imperfect technology of ratio conversion, even long-legged Cyd Charisse in *The Band Wagon* is made to look squat.

9

Doctor Opimian sets out once more to visit Mr Falconer with a view to inviting his participation in the Aristophanic comedy performance planned for the Grange.

The day was mild, enchanting as the smile
On certain painted saints, eyes raised towards the
heavens.

The day smiled elusively. Behind the curtain of sun-dappled trees, confidences and a general Confidence seemed imminent. Speculation or Fantasy need not venture far into the extraneous before one imagines the doctor's walk enlivened by encounters with a unicorn, a griffin, a wizard, an immovable object, the Single Actor from the earliest drama, a few Platonic Forms in search of a cave. One might even picture him equipped with a map on a scale bordering on parity which lists every ancient name for every rivulet, rise, declivity, outcrop, grove, ruins, standing stone. The Trickle of Russet, The Lightning Strike, The Glen of Content, Porson's Bridge, The Enigma, Half-way, Zeno's Last Stand.

At the Folly, Mr Falconer agreed to visit and take part in the play; and after the doctor's request to see other rooms hitherto hidden he was shown his host's bedroom decorated in tribute to Saint Catharine. Paintings in oils, stained-glass, decorative panels depicted the saint who, Mr Falconer explained, had been adopted as a testament to ideal beauty rather than mystifying faith.

But, thought the doctor, how pale and bloodless are depictions of the saints.

St Catharine is white as a sheet
From her face to the tips of her feet
    But perhaps extreme pallor
    Betokening valour
May seem meet to the man in the street.

Mr Falconer's fastidious idealism is expressed in a statement worth repeating at length:
"I wish to believe in the presence of some local spiritual influence; genius or nymph; linking us by a medium of something

like human feeling, but more pure and more exalted, to the all-pervading creative and preservative spirit of the universe; but I cannot realise it from things as they are. Everything is too deeply tinged with sordid vulgarity. There can be no intellectual power resident in a wood, where the only inscription is not '*Genio loci*', but 'Trespassers will be prosecuted'; no Naiad in a stream that turns a cotton-mill; no Oread in a mountain dell, where a railway train deposits a cargo of vandals; no Nereids or Oceanitides along the seashore, where a coastguard is watching for smugglers."

The two friends parted, mutually cheered by such sentiments and an enthusiasm for the forthcoming comedy.

10

Here at once must be incorporated, like a secondary thread in a weft shuttle to be hurled across the warp, the incident in *Sense and Sensibility* when Marianne is opportunely rescued by Willoughby – and, indeed, in *Pride and Prejudice* when Jane, chilled from a cloudburst, is obliged to recuperate in the Bingley household.

Morgana Gryll has ridden by coach and pair with her uncle to view the Folly after Doctor Opimian's glowing descriptions, and almost at its door they are struck by lightning. One of the horses is killed and Miss Gryll either injured or shocked sufficiently to have to remain at the Folly. She is accommodated in the female quarters and attended by the Seven Sisters. Meanwhile Mr Gryll and Dr Opimian – who has been visiting Mr Falconer at the time – having satisfied themselves of Morgana's comfort, enjoy a splendid and genial dinner.

The storm's an impressive machine
As grave as Giorgione's had been.
When she's thrown to the floor

Miss Gryll will need more
Than umbrellas as Fates intervene.

11

An erudite discussion of electricity, many aspects of which were known to the ancients. Here the doctor slips in frequent references to "Homer, Aeschylus, Aristotle, Plutarch, Athenaeus, Horace, Persius, and Pliny" in support of the assertion. The dubious value of more recent applications of the phenomenon is questioned – the nuisances occasioned by the electric telegraph, for example.

Here the discussion might easily have advanced to even more recent indulgences – the pervasiveness of the stuff, the search for fundamental particles, the hunting of the quark, sleep-overs at the edge of black holes, and in a modern transposition, a near-singularity where

> The Hadron Collider
> Sat down beside her
> And frightened Miss Gryll in her coach.

Or

> A charming young lady named Gryll
> Found in Nature the ultimate thrill.
>   As the storm turned skies white
>   And the horses took fright,
> She was caught in a long-sounding trill.

There are recuperative lunches in sunlight on the lawn:

The sun on our faces
The air like a swan
The forest in laces
With winter begun;

The shades of past summer
Conveyed on the wing
With a courteous glimmer
Still able to bring

Convivial pleasure
To the company at large
And discourse at leisure
Like a slow-moving barge.

Miss Gryll's complete recovery so ardently wished by all parties including Mr Falconer is nevertheless by him to be regretted, in that it signals her departure.

After this he resorts to the library, to the depictions of ideal beauty therein, including representations of the pale St Catharine. He is restless. Two hand-maidens of the seven serve luncheon and he is temporarily appeased. But soon afterwards, with a slashing stick and his dog (a companion animal to that of the doctor's) he plunges into the forest.

For one who tends to favour ideal pasts
Over present turbulent contingencies,
The forest with its ancient oaks appears
To offer solace. Here Maid Marian
Etc, etc.
"The forest depths through which Angelica fled"
Etc, etc.
Laura, Rosalind etc, etc.

And the sense of history is palpable.

The oak branches proffer their peace
Or, from sighs, sympathetic release
    Where calmed by the years
    In tiers after tiers
This turbulence may find surcease.

Still unassuaged however, Algernon Falconer returns. He is greatly disturbed by the intrusion of the real or, we might venture more recently to say, the hyper-real: the supervening of a real person with beating heart and pulse and infinitely variant gaze, on the wall frieze of the Ideal.

In the evening the Seven Sisters soothe him by musical offerings but he is still troubled – for he is a person who believes, or wants to believe, tranquillity superior to excitement. In this state of disquiet he is pleased one morning to greet Doctor Opimian. He adduces Pindar and the ninth Pythian ode in which Cyrene wrestles with the lion. He believes that love which encourages the lover to see everything through the imposed image of his mistress would be a disaster – a calamity not just in its effect on such perceptions but a mischance, a lightning strike to be avoided. He prefers the tranquillity of Wordsworth's "days so like each other they could not be remembered".

Like the oak tree unmoved in a glade
Not remembering each sequence of shade
    I would wish to remain
    Without love's bright pain
In the shadows, serene, undismayed.

He confides in Dr Opimian his susceptibility to the more than ideal beauty of Miss Morgana Gryll and his consequent reluctance to venture to the Grange. The married happiness of the Opimians is advanced by the doctor as a persuasion; further the charming presence of Lord Curryfin which might well deflect Miss Gryll's piercing gaze from the vulnerable Algernon.

A lengthy exchange of argument for and against the possibility of happiness in marriage ensues, with laughter and concessions from both sides. In the end Mr Falconer, as curious to see Lord Curryfin as he is wary of further exposure to the dangerous sunlight of Miss Gryll, agrees to go to the Grange.

13

Lord Curryfin's lecture on fish
Has his listeners all hooked, on a dish.
　　Each fingerling fact
　　Delivered with tact
Quite exceeds every fish-lover's wish.

The sight of Lord Curryfin's jaw
Makes the ladies inclined to adore.
　　His lectures on carp
　　To the strains of a harp
Have the erudite longing for more.

Lord Curryfin is crossing the country giving his lectures on fish. He is an accomplished young man who will court Miss Gryll before finally ceding the field to Mr Falconer in facilitating his own attachment to another. His talents are many; he has charm and daring. He is equal to the challenges of difficult figure skating, the taming of horses; he has brought a variety of inventions... He will single-handedly construct the stage-set for the Aristophanic comedy.

His talents and interests include
The sciences (where risks intrude),
   A hot air balloon
   Figure skating and, soon,
Whatever caprice suits his mood.

Lord Curryfin "with his usual desire to have a finger in every pie" has been invited to the Grange. Here he is struck by the startling beauty of the resident Miss Gryll. One might compare the following from Peacock's unfinished *Calidore* fragment – "Nature had gifted our youth with a very susceptible spirit, and the contemplation of this beautiful creature fanned the dormant sparks of his natural combustibility into an instantaneous conflagration."

14

The ladies leave the gentlemen to discussion over wine; Mr Falconer, deferring to the ancients, defends the Greek musical scales: he is not overfond of the piano since it is tuned in tempered or approximate scales and not natural harmonics; Mr MacBorrowdale is reluctant to be drawn on any subject other than the wine; the Reverend Doctor Opimian voices the important principle relating to realism in art: "I must take pleasure in the thing represented before I can derive any from the representation"; Mr Pallet discounts Mr Falconer's advocacy by scorning the lack of perspective in ancient art; a discussion of fools allows the doctor to castigate several classes of them, including the "competitive examination man who would not allow a drayman to lower a barrel into a cellar unless he could expound the mathematical principles by which he performed the operation".

Mr Falconer Silently Appeals to the Power of the Ancient Modes.

"The musical scales before the imposition
Of Just (or Contrived) Temperament – an art
Now lost to us – must have been prodigal
In the expression of a complete range
Of passions such as now I mutely suffer
Since Miss Gryll was struck by that same lightning
As that day struck me in meeting her."
                              – Algernon Falconer

Dinner at the Grange. Mr Gryll went in with Miss Ilex, a sympathetic older woman not previously mentioned, who will later regale Miss Gryll with confidences. Lord Curryfin went in with Miss Gryll, and Mr Falconer by misfortune found himself at the opposite end of the table from them.

15

Unexpectedness: Mr Falconer's excess of discomposure at seeing Lord Curryfin far away at table with Miss Gryll; Doctor Opimian's surprise at seeing Mr Falconer's preference for Miss Ilex over several other young ladies in the room; Miss Ilex's assertion that in respect of expression and "redundancy of ornament" Donizetti might be preferred to Mozart; Miss Gryll's rendering of *The Dappled Palfrey*, a ballad, which appears to cause agitation in Mr Falconer; unexpected modulations.

In *Headlong Hall*, by the author of *Gryll Grange*, unexpectedness is asserted as the quintessence of architecture.

By analogy, unexpectedness to be valued in narrative.

Fragment from an epistolary novel: a letter not sent.

"My dear Miss Gryll,
    When I heard – and saw – you lead *The Dappled Palfrey* gently into our midst I was greatly disturbed. Forgive me for resorting to redundancy of ornament but I must explain that previously I had, in the remoteness of the Tower, aspired to the serenity of the Mozartian in which temporal progress and retarding expression are in perfect accord; but you have plunged me into the turbulence of a Donizetti aria filled with sighs and protestations – " [to be continued]

Is her particular *timbre* best suited
To the clavicymbal or clavicytherium or clavicithern?
Lord Curryfin: On that I cannot pronounce
But it would certainly not be a clavicorn
Which is a species of clubhorned beetle.

After Miss Gryll's delightful performance of *The Dappled Palfrey* another young lady, rather more reserved in manner, sang the famous and affecting ballad, *Love and Age*.

16

Miss Alice Niphet, the young lady referred to, provides a counterweight to the attractions of Miss Gryll. Lord Curryfin is impressed. Peacock's concession to Southey, whom he has previously ridiculed: "Marble paleness suits her well."
    Miss Niphet is the only daughter of a gentleman living a few miles distant. She is to be the leader of the Chorus in the Aristophanic comedy. In conversation with her on the many topics on which he is an expert Lord Curryfin is impressed. Later she glimpses him struggling single-handedly with the stage set.

An Odd Perspective

Miss Niphet returning from walking outdoors
Saw Lord Curryfin high in the air,
Swinging backwards and forwards above the board stage
Then vanishing into the sky.

After this strange disappearance into the canvas heavens above the stage, at breakfast Miss Niphet could not prevent herself smiling.

Later at the lake — she in the pavilion to read, he to sail from the boathouse — the absurdity of his disappearance into that artificial blue ether had receded, to be replaced with a concern for his recklessness with boats.

Rehearsals proceed serendipitously. Lord Curryfin is drawn equally and differently to Miss Gryll and Miss Niphet, although there is the complication of a declaration made to the former.

Double Lime-rick

Lord Curryfin "happens" to meet
Miss Niphet each day by the lake.
She is reading of course, and discreet,
While he senses the trill and the shake
    In the air which each day
    With the sun through the trees
    Seems already to play
    Like the lake in a breeze
So their mornings continue to make
Arabesques overflowing, replete.

The rehearsals remind us distantly of the rehearsals for *Lovers' Vows* in *Mansfield Park*.

Idyllic Accident

The lake invited daring. Lord Curryfin,
Determined innovator that he was,
Invented an infallible new sail
Which at its first trial plunged him into the mere.
Showering water, shaking himself, he heard

Miss Niphet voice a gratifying concern
Then saw her blush. Impulsively he exclaimed,
"Surely till now I never looked on beauty!"
To which she almost said, then checked herself,
"Surely you have already looked on Miss Gryll."

Decisive Action

Miss Niphet, after the sail was brought to shore
And hoisted up to dry, set it on fire. "No more,"
She said as he surveyed the ashes in surprise,
"Will that sail ever cast you overboard in sighs."

17

Flared Nostrils

Lord Curryfin, expert in exciting praise
Took on himself next day the taming of a horse.

Miss Niphet seeing him from her window on the field
Felt great alarm, imagining the headlong rush

Past overhanging boughs. She hastened to the field,
Startled when he returned with fiery mount sedate.

Miss Niphet, marble Melpomene, suddenly
In tears, as suddenly ran like Atalanta.

Flux

At breakfast Melpomene seemed impassive; at rehearsals she performed but was remote, and departed at once afterwards. By the lake Lord Curryfin found the pavilion empty. He asked himself how it could be that he had so recently proposed to Miss Gryll when he was now eager to propose to Miss Niphet. He could not be sure at what stage of incipience or development love was eddying some distance out from shore. He could not be sure the sail was infallible.

Similarly Mr Falconer felt the anchor of the Seven Sisters and their offer of an endless Mozartiana weighing against the impulse in the sail to test the breeze offshore. Miss Gryll felt divided between the Apollonian Algernon and the Dionysian Lord Curryfin.

Only Miss Niphet seemed set on a clear course. After finding Lord Curryfin merely amusing, she now found herself troubled by his attentions to Miss Gryll.

The pavilion was deserted still and filled with shadows,
Lord Curryfin felt its emptiness echo in himself.
But suddenly Melpomene appeared. She took his hand.
"My maid informs me you intend to try that dangerous horse
In harness and in some high phaeton you've invented
With thus a double chance to break your neck ...
I entreat you therefore to abandon your intentions."

Lord Curryfin assured her of the infallibility of his invention and his power over horses but that, if she denied him this present course, it was a small sacrifice to abstain from certain projects.

"And from sailing boats?"

"From sailing boats."

"And from balloons?"

"From balloons? But what suggested balloons? As a matter of fact I *have* thought of balloons and I have invented an infallible valve – "

Lord Curryfin Reins In

My inventions are somewhat erratic
But of one thing I am most emphatic –
If you say "No balloon!"
I'll be down to earth soon;
My New-Leaf-Turning-Over's dramatic.

Having secured his promises in the matter of horses, carriages, sails, balloons, Miss Niphet was delighted to see his resourcefulness employed in the invention of acoustic devices for the theatre.

Sonority in the Athenian Theatre

Lord Curryfin now turned his attention to the study of sonorous vases as proposed by Vitruvius, whereby the harnessing of Harmonics allowed these to be placed round the theatre to increase sonority. He had made a number of such vases only to find at their first trial a gong-like, intolerable roaring resulted.

The roaring of amplified sea-shells
When supplying a surrogate sea
Now accompanied the slightest stage whisper
And threatened expediency.

The modern reader might recall Gogol's story in which, in order to hide squalid streets from the impending visit of an important government official, screens are erected around the town square

– resulting in a roar of echoes as soon as the mayor's speech of welcome is begun.

The principle of amplification suggests also the exquisite phenomenon found rarely near waterfalls where a cave in the vicinity has the form of a parabola, so that when one approaches the parabola's focal point the rays of sound from the falls are focussed there. The result is a splendid enlargement and concentration of the roar of water.

Lord Curryfin was discouraged. Miss Niphet was more positive, cheered by two facts: first that though intolerably noisy the vases could always be removed, and second, that this unsolved problem kept the inventor from more dangerous pursuits.

18

To test the acoustics of the theatre (with the vases discreetly removed) the participants gave a series of lectures: Lord Curryfin (Fish), Mr Minim (Music), Mr Pallet (Painting), Mr MacBorrowdale (Foreign Affairs). Mr Falconer spoke on Domestic Life in Homer, Mr Gryll on Epicureanism, and Doctor Opimian, rather than subject the company to his usual fare, recited a long-ish version of a poem on Chivalry.

19

General debate on diverse topics. The electric telegraph is dismissed as regrettable if it facilitates communication with Americans. Other aspects of technical innovation deplored. Mr Gryll proposes Newfoundland salt fish as a possible counter-argument in favour of exchange with Americans but Dr Opimian holds to the view that this benefit is greatly outweighed by other factors less favourable. The conversation is lengthy. Mr

MacBorrowdale voices scepticism as to the benefit of lectures on any topic. Dr Opimian returns to his particular dislike – Competitive Examiners, whose precept he takes to be, "It is better to learn to gabble about everything than to understand anything".

20

Algernon and Morgana

Winter fields; an early heavy frost; the window and winter light; austere backdrops to the comedy; Miss Gryll reading, quite alone; Mr Falconer at the door.

> The whiteness of winter enhances
> The earnest demeanour of glances.
> In light strangely sweet
> Their slow gazes meet
> With the force of a thousand hurled lances.

Algernon enters.

Morgana has been reading *Orlando Innamorata* after whose enchantress she has been named. Courteous greetings are exchanged. "Diffugere nives" hangs faintly on the air – confirming that traces of the past persist. She reads aloud the passage in which her namesake offers the golden lock of hair which Orlando, missing the opportunity, fails to seize. Similarly Algernon is diffident, uncertain, hesitant, and lets the moment pass without making the declaration which both sense as imminent.

Instead they speak of Morgana's other suitor. She has rejected many, but this present contender – they agree – is mercurial, inventive and malleably eager to please. Yet she finds something lacking in his character which she cannot explain. Algernon notes with generosity his humour and title as advantages. Then slipping out of the sevenfold protection of the Seven Sisters, he ventures a compliment. Morgana blushes. The sevenfold bands are loosened. An understanding or declaration might have occurred had not an interruption prevented it.

After failing at this hurdle Algernon returns through the woods by postilion, and regains at that leisurely gait a measure of serenity, a sort of cushion to place over the horns of his dilemma. He is alarmed at the thought of Morgana becoming Lady Curryfin; his reverie inclines him towards the declaration he did not make. Yet the prospect of the Seven Sisters greeting him and providing music is calming. He is again in the evenly poised dilemma of Rasselas — "the wants of him who wants nothing". He watches the familiar patterns of the woods slowly passing.

In winter's chief beauty, the woods,
The rime frost persists in its glades.
The cold sound of hooves
On the bare ground approves
The loud indecision of birds.

At the Grange a learned discussion ensues on the identification of fossils. Lord Curryfin notes "that petrifactions were often siliceous but never pure silex," an observation not acknowledged by Mr MacBorrowdale.

The distant tower, the calming power of seven,
The charm of indecisive Algernon ...

The lake was frozen solid. On the ice
Lord Curryfin performed and, in a trice,
Had dazzled all admirers on the shore.

Miss Niphet joins him, and is as like Atalanta on ice as formerly on the lawns. Exertion brings a flush to her cheeks, and Lord Curryfin observes that he now sees absolute confirmation that the Athenians preferred their marble statuary tinted.

> The ice is as white as her face
> As she skates with a consummate grace.
> Yet her cheeks bear a flush
> Which is not quite a blush –
> She's like marble with rose carapace.

The skaters are admired by Miss Gryll, Miss Ilex and Doctor Opimian.

Another Dilemma

Miss Gryll watches admiringly this gliding pair, who, Doctor Opimian observes, seem so close as to suggest Jupiter's creation of apt couples subsequently divided and set in search of one another. Miss Gryll senses that Lord Curryfin's ardour towards her has perhaps declined into deference; she has deflected his declaration in the greater flame of Algernon's presence but that presence has evaporated and he is again in an extended retreat in the tower with the Seven.

Miss Gryll and Miss Niphet Muse
A Ballad of Attachments

> We are two friends. We admire each other.
> We love Lord Curryfin as a brother.
> – And yet in Morgana I see a light
> Like light in a house approached at night.

– And yet in Alice I see reserve
Like a screen of trees behind which curve
The lights of a coach drawing up at dawn
From which steps down and crosses the lawn

A stranger preceding a shimmering breeze
Who waves and calls to one upstairs.
We are two friends. We share one thing:
We both find Curryfin interesting.

We walk beside the frozen lake
And at its centre for our sake
He skates where summer saw him sail
Aboard the good ship Fallible.

And whether Curryfin sink or swim
Or ride a rampant stallion tame
Or swing above the stage-set scrim
We two friends think the world of him.

Yet another who strides the firmament
Is altogether more diffident;
Morgana sees the light from the tower
And recognises its curious power

Where a sevenfold secret Sisterhood
Suggesting starshine Pleiadic cloud
Hangs like a shadow round that sun...
There in his library Algernon,

Sheltering in Ideality
Is protected from the whelming sea;
And two friends ponder what is meant
In the gaze of this charming diffident.

We are two friends. We are Miss Gryll
And Melpomene or, if you will,
Miss Alice Niphet – both as perplexed
Not knowing whom to favour next.

And yet we are confident calm will prevail
And by Christmas snows will each regale
The other with triumphal calm
When each of our lovers finds his home.

22

As Christmas approaches, Doctor Opimian reflects on the
iconography and associations and rituals and pleasures of that
season; halcyon, hearth, holly, mistletoe, sausage, plum-pudding
– oblate as the earth's sphere – punch, roast, yule-log. His reverie
is interrupted by a knock at the door. It is Harry Hedgerow who
asks the doctor's help and intervention and advice in his suit and
that of six companions. Harry has proposed to Dorothy without
success; the other six wish to marry her sisters. All are thwarted
by the hermit of the Folly, Mr Falconer. But now they hear that
he is to marry Miss Gryll. This being so they wish to press forward
into the resulting vacuum and request the doctor's advocacy. Dr
Opimian is hopeful but uncertain. He questions whether there is
any dispute amongst the six as to their selections. But –

Each of the seven rustics is by serendipity
Enamoured of a different sister,
Against all probability.
"That," says Harry, "is the beauty of it."

23

Returning after an absence to the Grange, Mr Falconer observes what he assumes to be Miss Gryll's renewed interest in Lord Curryfin.

In the Arena of the Quadrille

There are two quadrilles: a) the dance and b) the card game – more convivial and less ill-tempered than whist. In the former Lord Curryfin excels. With Miss Niphet he surpasses all others. Mr Falconer, who does not dance, notes what he takes to be a glistening – jealousy construes it as a tear – in Miss Gryll's eye. He questions himself ceaselessly; he reproaches himself repeatedly for his failure to declare himself, to seize the golden lock when it was offered.

> Could this glistening be really a tear
> Like a glimmering sword in the mere
> Which condemns my inaction
> And futile distraction
> And causes this shimmering fear?

While Mr Falconer trudges through the drear land of Near-And-Yet-So-Far, Doctor Opimian, Miss Ilex, Mr Gryll and Mr MacBorrowdale play cards – the relaxed game of Quadrille – an excellent opportunity for a discussion of truth to Nature in several writers. Pope is mildly cautioned by Miss Ilex for errors in his account of the card game in *The Rape of the Lock*. Wordsworth, Milton and Burns are praised for the accuracy of their observation. The same cannot be said for Moore, who is severely censured for illogic; and Moore fares no better, in Doctor Opimian's view, in his account of Cleopatra's complexion.

All this while Miss Niphet has been the cynosure and

culmination in the dance, while Mr Falconer sinks into greater Stygian marshes to reflect on his disappearance at a critical moment, his failure to declare himself to Miss Gryll. He has stayed away for too long.

Miss Gryll now planned ways of overcoming the young man's irresolution, his retreat into the fortress provided by the Seven Sisters, which she feared without her intervention would be of long duration.

> She considered the deployment of her power
> To bring the dreamer closer to the hour.

24

> Outside, the snow fell through the night
> And morning seemed wide-eyed in white;
> Lord Curryfin went out to skate
> And Mr Falconer looked for Miss Gryll.

> She sat serenely in a shade,
> *Orlando* open at her side.
> "You have been long away," she said.
> He heard the waxwing's distant trill.

At this there begins the long circuitous manoeuvre in which both celebrants with artless art act out their roles. Morgana begins by reporting Doctor Opimian's opinion concerning the sevenfold improbability that he – Mr Falconer – would return. Algernon protests his desire to ask her forgiveness without assuming that which he has no right to assume. She offers to supply the assertion – presumed in this assumption – which she might put into his mouth, this being conditional upon his making no reply for four times seven days. He agrees to the condition. She provides him with the declaration which he should have made when the volume of *Orlando Innamorata* first lay open at the proffered lock of hair. Placing her finger over her lips she waits his assenting silence, then says "You will resolve to speak only after four times seven days and if not then, never."

> Not to utter for twenty-eight days
> The least word of irresolute praise,
> > But to wrestle with fate,
> > Then to pass through the gate
> And traverse without baulk this bright maze.

The twenty-eight days of silence already exerted their weight.

> He feared still Lord Curryfin;
> He walked into the park's snow court,
> Resigned to wait in restless doubt
> For twenty-eight days of snow-filled thought.

25

Meanwhile Harry Hedgerow was executing a manoeuvre of his own. To Dorothy he said, "What if the master were to marry? And what if the new Lady Falconer were to take control of the house? What then? What if all your sisters were to marry?" "In these unlikely events, then it would be you I would think of, Harry Hedgerow."

26

A weary time; there passed a weary time.

At dinner Lord Curryfin went in with Miss Gryll and many miles away at the opposite end of the table sat Mr Falconer with Miss

Niphet. A silence largely ensued between these two, cast away as they were into a remote and ill-lit corner of the world. Mr Falconer endeavoured from a distance to analyse every aspect of the gaiety Miss Gryll displayed to the affable Lord Curryfin, who, if not entertaining the company about fish was equally beguiling on a veritable kaleidoscope of other subjects. From their remote vantage Miss Niphet was perhaps more confident than Mr Falconer.

> Once again he is out in the snow
> And with twenty-eight days still to go
>   He is snow-blind already
>   And feeling unsteady
> With Morgana far off on a floe.

> Mr Falconer's hopes put to flight
> He is plunged in perpetual night
>   And for twenty-eight days
>   Must endure Cupid's rays
> While Morgana fades almost from sight.

27

Love in Memory
A Song

> Love in Memory is no less
> Than love Still Present. One's a field,
> The other is a library.

> In the field the present floats
> Above star-flowers in the grass
> And love is like its fragrant air;

While in the library it waits
In pages opened long ago
And still as fresh when opened now,

As light brims at the constant glass.
For both project an ideal face
And catalogue shared history;

And both are as concerned as snow
On windless mornings when the field
And library window scan the sky.

The song is performed by Miss Gryll and Miss Ilex. Morgana confides in Miss Ilex her device for bringing Mr Falconer to decisive action; Miss Ilex compliments her on her resolution and confesses that once, long ago, she lacked similar determination and that as a result ...

The History of Miss Ilex in Summary

In the labyrinth set with trees
Where every fair face seems to please
There is no single path
To a warm, waiting hearth
And romance may disperse in the breeze.

i.e. In the wild woods lovely with trees
It seems he gave her the breeze.

Miss Ilex gives her grave and touching account of her lover who wandered in the woods of affection upon affection, and could not find any point of repose in the labyrinth. She for her part showed too great a reticence and waited for his decision which never came. She applauds Morgana's resolve to force the young man to focus the beams of his intentions … *Convergence is all.* "He would disappear for weeks at a time, wandering in forests, climbing mountains, and descending into dingles of mountain-streams, with no other companions than a large Newfoundland dog…"

"Why!" exclaimed Miss Gryll, "that is a very like description of our author and his dog Luath."

28

The Aristophanic Comedy

The theatre's the place for illusion
Beneficial for mental contusion
    Where to see spirits fly
    Or events long gone by
Time and space breed delightful confusion.

Thaw and drying wind, the roads favourable, the fifth day of Christmas appointed for the Aristophanic comedy.

Brilliant candlelight in chandeliers illumines the gallery, argon lamps cast a mysterious milklight on the stage.

The scene opens on rooms of the Spirit Rapping Society. Circe and Gryllus who have been sleeping for three thousand years – "a nap indeed" – stir. Their observations on the present state of Society are distinctly unfavourable.

Three spirit-rappers enter with table. Circe and Gryllus summoned. They are still ill-disposed towards what they see.

To persuade Gryllus otherwise a Chorus of Clouds is summoned – "a dazzling array of female beauty revealed by degrees through misty gauze." They invoke a pageant of Reformers. Gryllus is unimpressed.

Enter seven Competitive Examiners. Their inquisition of

candidates proceeds. Several admirably qualified, including Hannibal and Richard Coeur-de-Lion, are rejected. Gryllus is unimpressed. Richard Coeur-de-Lion raises his battle-axe over the heads of the examiners, who are put to flight.

The Chorus summon further tableaux depicting advances in science and gadgetry. Gryllus detects absurdities in each. The spirit-rappers object that he is predisposed to prefer tranquillity to excitement, and insist on the splendours of progress.

Thunderous laughter offstage proves to be that of Jupiter. The table-turning accelerates; table legs dance, chair arms pinch the spirit-rappers and pursue them offstage. Lord Curryfin's stage invention is here a triumph of ingenuity in contrast with the fiasco of the sonorous vases.

Before returning, Gryllus and Circe concede that one aspect of the modern world may be worthwhile, namely, the gastronomic. A splendid supper is served. Gryllus is impressed.

Miss Gryll's performance as Circe delighted Mr Falconer; Lord Curryfin admired particularly Miss Niphet as leader of the Chorus. "The supper passed off joyously and it was a late hour of the morning before the company dispersed."

29

A week later a ball is to be held. Mr Falconer retreats for the period of his enforced silence to the Tower. Here the Seven Sisters provide some measure of distraction. At the Grange the discussions continue. The veracity of the tradition of the Bald Venus is questioned by Doctor Opimian. While the doctor expatiates on first love, Lord Curryfin is encouraged by Miss Niphet's animation at battledore and shuttlecock.

30

Noting her fatigue Lord Curryfin at last catches the shuttlecock in his hand in order to terminate a prodigiously long rally.

In the secluded drawing room Alice Niphet and Morgana Gryll seal their friendship in a long conversation of great empathy. Morgana, recognising that her friend is undoubtedly attached in affection to Lord Curryfin declares she would release him from any trace of obligation he may still retain from his earlier declaration.

This she does, and Lord Curryfin in turn loses no time in seeking out Miss Niphet. They agree joyfully to use the names Richard and Alice forthwith.

31

Twelfth Night; the ball; Richard and Alice revelling in country dances, waltzes and minuets; Miss Gryll who might seem to have lost two suitors in one day was nonetheless not lacking partners; the Twelfth Night cake apportioned; a discussion of domestic cookery and numerous other matters; amongst participants in a Quadrille (the dance), Miss Niphet's transformation from marble beauty to animated beauty was universally noted; punch was enjoyed by the gentlemen and "not absolutely disregarded by the young ladies."

> As Alice and Richard performed a quadrille
> And the Twelfth Night cake was apportioned to all,
> While admirers surrounded Miss Gryll in a whirl,
> Far off in a tower's pale hall
> A hymn to Saint Catharine was weaving its pall.

32

On his way to the Tower, Doctor Opimian met Harry Hedgerow. The Siege of The Seven Against Thebes, proceeding as well as it might, is dependent only on the capricious citadel and capstone of Mr Falconer, a citadel which might yet fall.

Walking on alone, the doctor ruminated. He is concerned for Miss Gryll. Perhaps she should have pursued the attachment of Lord Curryfin. And yet Miss Niphet and he are admirably suited. And Miss Gryll seems now cast adrift at the pleasure of the gods. And Mr Falconer has been silent – and notably absent in the Tower.

Close to his destination the doctor encounters Mr Falconer pacing in anxious haste. The two walk on to the Tower eagerly conversing. Asked what he has been reading, Mr Falconer points to an edition of *Orlando Innamorata*. The doctor observes that he has recently seen the same text open at the Grange, but stops short of remarking on sympathy of taste.

Doctor Opimian has resolved to avoid the subject of Miss Gryll, while Mr Falconer is anxious for every and any mention of her, so as to speak of his contract of silence. The doctor almost veers towards the subject only to be distracted by a chance reference to Thor and Odin which blossoms into a very long excursus – across which Mr Falconer finally plunges and speaks of Morgana.

The Seven Sisters are an impediment. Were they his own sisters there would be no problem. Unfortunately marriage – even to the most indulgent or enlightened woman – could only increase the impediment of excessive feminine scruple in the Tower.

> The Seven Sisters like emerging stars
> Seem strangely an impediment to the moon.

The doctor ventures the suggestion that the marriage of all seven to suitable suitors might just be the solution.

33

Mr Falconer sent for Dorothy and, propelled by her modest eagerness, sent for Harry Hedgerow. Their discussion advanced with a delighted acceleration towards its natural end: complete sympathetic agreement and the suggestion that Dorothy, at present without a fortune, should arrive at the altar with a handsome settlement.

34

On the twenty-seventh day of his probation Mr Falconer returned to the Grange with a light heart. But before the twenty-eighth day can bestow its long awaited resolution there must be interposed a recital of ghost stories – in accordance with the tradition of their narration at Christmas. And so the evening is prolonged by a succession of them, many touching on the notable characteristic of such tales – that on the highroad or in the woods some strange and fearful event occurs, some feature of which is repeated like an echo or anomaly when the traveller returns. Thus Dr Opimian, for example, recounts from Petronius the story of a man who sees his companion on the road turn into a wolf; the wolf enters a farm and attacks sheep but is driven off by a spear through the neck. Then on his return the man finds his companion in the care of a surgeon who is dressing a wound in his neck.

In turn Miss Gryll, Miss Ilex, Mr Falconer, Mr MacBorrowdale and Mr Gryll recount tales peopled by sepulchres, ghostly lute-playing, witches, solemn music, buried treasure, shadows cast by moonlight etc., etc. Mr Falconer concludes proceedings by a ghostly ballad about an incorruptible Saint Laura.

35

A resolution devoutly to be wished may often approach, and, by a curious acceleration in time, seem scarcely to be about to happen before it is being celebrated by admirers and well-wishers. Thus no detailed account is given of the happy end to the embargo on vital discussion between Morgana and Algernon, for "there was little to be said but that little was conclusive".

Instead of intruding upon this very private dialogue, more rewarding perhaps to imagine than to recount, the text occupies itself with the delight felt by Mr Gryll – which takes the form of his enquiring why she rejected various former suitors. The inventory of her responses makes a pleasing resumé of male inadequacies from which Mr Falconer is charmingly free.

And so we have in a kind of unlikely multiplication – beyond all reasonable bounds – of the twin weddings which end *Sense and Sensibility* and, one supposes, many a lesser romance, the simultaneous dispatch into bliss and contentment of nine couples. Lord Curryfin and Miss Niphet, Mr Falconer and Miss Gryll (with just the tantalising remains of the notion that these pairings might even have been reversed) and, bringing up the rear, Harry Hedgerow and his Dorothy with a supporting cast of six more sisters and six more swains. All arrive at the Grange to the good wishes of the company. Even Mrs Opimian emerges (like Mrs Elton at the end of *Emma* – though rather more generous than she) – to comment favourably. And the Reverend Doctor Opimian in his speech wishes them all, as is so often appropriate on such occasions, happiness and good fortune equal to his own.

Loose Ends

To the reader who has read the preceding pages but has not read *Gryll Grange* by Thomas Love Peacock ... *Are you mad?* Or, to be more constructive, shouldn't you at once give up everything non-essential and read it *at once?* Allowing time for say, an egg salad, a massage, a few hours sleep, a brief visit to the gym or a short tram ride along the sea coast, the entire book should take, let us say, two days, time eminently well spent. And to the reader who has lightly skimmed or even just leafed through the preceding pages – that is to say, most readers – it is to be hoped that you will read *Gryll Grange* by Thomas Love Peacock with considerably more attention.

There are within its gentle pages several significant platforms for bemusement. One is the notion of the wild woods (to import into proceedings Mr Badger presiding in dressing gown), woods extending from the Grange to the Tower which Doctor Opimian and Mr Falconer both traverse several times. Suggestions of the gold-leaf chiaroscuro of Samuel Palmer have already been mentioned. Doctor Opimian, with his inexhaustible curiosity about the arcane, might find somewhere along its twisting path reminders of several alternative traditions including that of the *tarantella*, that dance thought to be caused by the tarantula's bite but later supposed to be its cure: the dancer exerts a frenzy quite foreign to English mode of eccentric reflection, exemplified in conversation at the Grange. Imagine the doctor encountering such a dancer in the woods. What then? Or might the doctor encounter amongst certain mysterious trees whose language he cannot decipher, birds not native to these woods, the whip-bird from south-eastern Australia for example, or the South American hoopoe? What then?

Such *dislocation* or *unlikeliness* carries its own particular aesthetic force. What if (one might run on in imagination to suppose) Mr Falconer through restlessness or boredom in the library were to invite the Sisters to accompany him *outdoors*, there to experience botany, cell growth, the secrets of genetic variation, acids subsiding with ripeness into sugars, the occasional Darwinian adaptation, bird calls, extraordinary weather, crepitation – even a peculiar, never-before-heard music from the woods akin to the presence of *Sirens*? Or suppose that he goes one day to a nearby village fair with all of the Seven and dances with them?

Put the case – to use the memorable gambit from *Great Expectations* of Dickens (a writer Peacock enjoyed in old age, favouring *Our Mutual Friend* over *The Pickwick Papers*) – that Mr Falconer is actually in love with Dorothy, or that Mrs Opimian's suspicions, namely that goings-on are going on at the Folly, are well-founded. Or that one day Mr Falconer while plunging into a different part of the woods notices language on the move (like moving clouds perhaps gathering and regrouping) into *oddity*.

Or the stratospheric improbability that as Lord Curryfin endeavours to prolong the rally a particularly wayward stroke of the shuttlecock from Miss Niphet sends him to the wall where he sees a graffito he hasn't noticed before – "I ♥ Miss Nymphet".

Such extremities might also suggest that Lord Curryfin's inventiveness could also have led, given world enough and time, to such world-benefiting innovations as

a) The "Moving Retention Image" (or Cinema); "Noting the fact that the retina struggles for a slight interval to shrug off its captive image, a device might be contrived which transmits light through an image engraved on a glass lozenge; further, imagine a machine by which a succession of such lozenges are passed before a lantern."

b) "Rapid Walking on Water" (Water Ski-ing) with the possibility of a single ski for the intrepid.

c) A dirigible or navigable air balloon.

d) Electricity, known to the ancients and available in lightning, to be captured for domestic use – a splendid notion – and a subject suitable to succeed fish as a touring lecture.

e) An electrical musical instrument – perhaps in which the performer interferes with the electrical flow by interposing himself.

In such a mode of supposition, imagine that one evening at the Grange (in the manner of *La Boutique Fantasque*) the characters in *Gryll Grange* decide to act out an Aristophanic comedy *about him*, thus:

A Life of Thomas Love Peacock
As Enacted by the Grange Players

The players are Miss Ilex, Miss Gryll, Miss Niphet, Mr Falconer, Mr Gryll, Doctor and Mrs Opimian, Lord Curryfin – who has dropped in by yet-to-be-invented Dirigible. Cuckoos trill, finches chirr, nuthatches hatch a plot.

Scene 1

Miss Ilex: Thomas was a remarkably beautiful child.
    Queen Charlotte stopped in her carriage,
    Stopped and bent to kiss the young child.

Mrs Opimian: He has powerful eyes
    And will never wear spectacles
    Despite being a prodigious reader.

Miss Gryll: We summon the ghost of Fanny Falkiner.

Mr Falconer: They met in the ruins of Newark Abbey.

Lord Curryfin: Fanny and I have become engaged.

Miss Niphet: We have become engaged.
                He has taken a lock of my hair.
                He wears it in a locket.

Mr Gryll: Fanny's parents have decided otherwise.

Dr Opimian: Remember Coleridge's letter to Sara Hutchinson
                Written from the peak of Skidaw,
                Filled with longing.

Music in the Key of A Minor sounds.

Scene 2 *Lord Curryfin waves a wand invented for the occasion.*
The scene becomes their author's library. Enter Edith, Peacock's
grand-daughter.

Miss Gryll: Edith was the only human allowed
                To visit freely this dry vanilla library air,
                These gilt and leather vistas,
                These pages of subsumption and argument,
                These echoes, these splendid incursions, these
                        neologisms.

Lord Curryfin waves a trout rod and declaims.

Lord Curryfin: This week's Word of the Week
                Is *Jeremytaylorically*,
                A word I believe invented by our author.

Music in natural harmonics sounds. Miss Niphet steps up to the
lectern.

Miss Niphet: Edith reported many years later

That in his last weeks
After the disastrous library fire
He had recurring dreams of Fanny Falkiner.

Scene 3 *A backdrop of Welsh mountains.*

Miss Gryll: He meets Jane Gryffidh
            She is in love with him
            But he makes no sign.

Mr Gryll: With Doctor Gryffidh
            He went at midnight
            To view the Black Cataract.

Dr Opimian: But sadly for Jane Gryffidh
            There intervened the landslide and aurora and
               sunshowers
            Of Miss Marianne de St Croix.

Lord Curryfish plays natural harmonics on a hastily improvised trumpet.

Miss Gryll: Miss Marianne de St Croix
            Was as intriguing as her name.

Miss Niphet: And Jane Gryffidh vanished like sunlight in a
               forest
            And was obliged to wait in shadow.

Scene 4 *A waterfall*

Lord Curryfin: In 1812 our author had met Shelley;
              The poet was 20, Peacock 30.
              Shelley's enthusiasm was in full flood.

Producing inventions at a prodigious pace.

Miss Niphet:	Our author had called Jane Gryffidh "The Caevnavonshire Nymph".
Miss Gryll:	And Shelley named her "The milk white Snowdonian antelope." At this time Shelley was pursuing The sixteen year-old Mary Godwin.

Miss Niphet: And was about to abandon his wife Harriet.

Miss Ilex: And our author was dazzled by Marianne de St Croix.

Scene 5 *A Storm – Lord Curryfin supplies stage thunder by hurling sonorous vases to the floor.*

Miss Ilex: After a breach with Miss St Croix
            Sees an end to the Caprices of Marianne –

Miss Gryll: Our onlie true begetter
            Proposes to Jane Gryffidh by letter
            Not having seen her for eight years.
            The couple had a son and three daughters.

Miss Niphet: The second daughter died in 1826
            Occasioning great sadness
            And the couple adopted a cottage child
            Because of her resemblance to their lost daughter.

Scene 6 *The library. Subdued light. A spirit-rapping. A great many voices issue from the shelves. One – that of Edith – prevails.*

The voice of Edith:

> A fire broke out here
> In the library of his house on the Thames.
> He was injured in his attempt to save books.
> In his last weeks
> He had recurring dreams of Fanny Falkiner.

Curtain

And now Elaboration, already swimming dangerously beyond the breakers of the Arbitrary, reaches the outer sea of Irrevelance. For, in a parallel universe somewhere near you in a forest glade resembling that between Gryll Grange and the Folly, a reading group is picnicking. Lord Cucumber, the Earl of Mercury, Doctor and Mrs Linguini, Genevieve Angle, Miss Artmiss, Miss Argot & Henry Lancelot have met to discuss *Gryll Grange* and a body of musings about it. In between sandwiches and cordial, and speculations about technologies not yet invented – teleporting being their favourite – they are sifting through a pile of papers secured against the breeze by the picnic hamper.

Lord Cucumber: "Here's an unfinished lime-rick. It's about the lovely Morgana.

> Morgana at first was named Circe
> But Peacock, rethinking, showed mercy,
> And intelligent grace,
> So replete in her face,
> . . . ."

His fellow picnickers search for similar unconsidered trifles. Mrs Linguini: "Here's something. It says here, 'Even approaching the age of 80, the author's gastronomic proclivities were undiminished'".

Henry Lancelot (scrabbling):   "Do we have anywhere a likeness of Edith, his grand-daughter?"

The Earl of Mercury (reads): "Rising in the dirigible of his prose over the floodplain of events –"

Genevieve Angle: "Who wrote this stuff?"

Miss Artmiss (suddenly distracted): "It is clear Euclid's postulates are awry, particularly in relation to parallels. For here we are in a parallel universe, supposedly non-intersecting, yet, surely, the folly visible above the trees is that of Algernon Falconer. And the faces at the window, seven in number – "

"Why yes!" joins in Doctor Linguini, "It is Dorothy and her sisters, trying on their wedding finery."

Lord Cucumber: "Nevertheless we are here and seemingly unencumbered, and I urge that we resolve to continue indefinitely the pursuit of digression – for, as has been wisely said, 'No-one likes a didact.' And if we are – with tea and cakes – to celebrate happy endings, we should begin."

Notes

The *Peal of Bells* opens with the opening words of *A Sentimental Journey*, and a little later, touches on its famous closing sentence, "So that when I stretched out my hand..." Sterne is also present several more times: The Widow Wadman; the invitation to review the auxiliary verbs; the alphabetical list; the Tristrapaedia.

"Be a football to time and chance": Emerson.

"Books give not wisdom": Sir John Harington, *Epigrams*.

"Unconsidered trifles": Shakespeare, as is of course, "coldly furnished forth."

"*No! In Thunder*": Leslie Fiedler's exhortation to affirm excellence by denouncing mediocrity.

"The cement of the world" J. Mackie's term for causation as treated by Hume.

Brewer: *Dictionary of Phrase and Fable*, at the entry 'rats.'

Amongst the raised banners, mention of "Gallimaufrical Glasgow" refers to Bill's extensive research into Emblem Books there.

The cadential visitors leaning from their cloudy barouche are, to judge from their travels, Fielding, Smollett, Johnson, Sterne and Swift, all in Bill's particular pantheon.

"Length is my greatest Disgust": Richardson.

Confetti contains passages from *The Young Visitors* and *Tristram Shandy*; and the *Family Album* draws on information kindly supplied by Bill and Marcia's daughter, Sue.

The *Gryll Grange* synopsis preserves the content of the numbered chapters in the original.

The images throughout are taken from Emblem Books. These medieval or Renaissance picture books are philosophical, enigmatic, moral – in short, Maidmentian. They are generally collections of pictures, each with accompanying motto and verse gloss. Bill spoke of them often, for they had become a major interest, leading him to Glasgow, Paris and London. Their images contain strange mythologies, conjunctions of opposites, anthropomorphisms, symbolic conflations, intimations of mortality and immortality — attempts, it might seem, to say the unsayable, which is somewhat akin to reading the Maidment Smile of Reason.

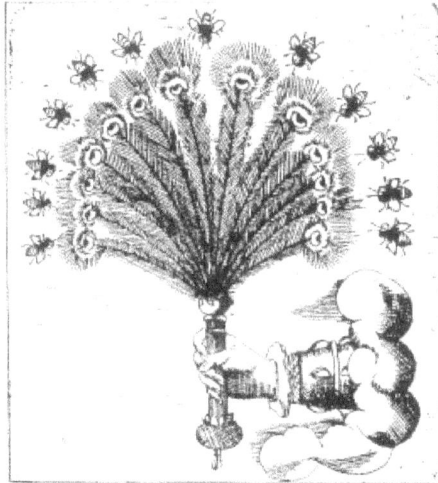